D1382900

I D E A

I N T O

I M A G E

ERIK HORNUNG

IDEA

Essays on Ancient

INTO

Egyptian Thought

IMAGE

Translated by Elizabeth Bredeck

TIMKEN PUBLISHERS

LIBRARY OF CONGRESS CATALOGING-IN-PUBLICATION DATA
Hornung, Erik.
    [Geist der Pharaonenzeit. English]
    Idea into image : essays on ancient Egyptian thought /
Erik Hornung ; translated by Elizabeth Bredeck.
        p.   cm.
    Translation of: Geist der Pharaonenzeit.
    Includes bibliographical references.
    ISBN 0-943221-11-0 : $25.00
    1. Philosophy, Egyptian.   I. Title.
B141.H6713   1992
181'.2—dc20   91-46855
                                                CIP

Type set in Granjon and Univers by Wilsted & Taylor
Designed by David Bullen
Copyedited by Anna Jardine
Printed by Princeton University Press Printers

Frontispiece and Back jacket: The sky goddess Nut with her
name in the sun disk on her head; inside surface of the Dynasty
26 coffin of Udjaersen, The Metropolitan Museum of Art,
New York.

Front jacket: Detail of a head from an undecorated Late Period
outer coffin, The Metropolitan Museum of Art, New York.

HEINO GÄFGEN

*In thanks for many years of friendship and
stimulation, and in memory of the first trip
to Egypt in 1956*

THIS book is a translation of Erik Hornung's *Geist der Pharaonenzeit*, published in 1989. The purpose of that book, and of this translation, is to make ancient Egyptian ideas available to an audience with no special background in Egyptology. Most of the chapters originated as lectures. Three chapters that were in the German edition have been dropped because the publisher felt they were not at the same level as the other chapters. The bibliographical notes from the German edition are translated here, but no attempt has been made to amplify them with information on English language material. The English edition includes numerous black-and-white illustrations that elucidate specific points in the text. The photographs used as chapter openings have been selected not with a view to illustrating the text, but rather because they provide a glimpse of the human beings behind ancient Egyptian ideas. The publisher thanks Bill Barrette for providing most of the photographs, and Christine Lilyquist for her editorial help.

CONTENTS

IDEA

INTO

IMAGE

For authors of antiquity, Egypt was where philosophy began, a source of wisdom. Egyptian culture was an ancient one, with traditions reaching back to the start of history. Along with the Sumerians, the Egyptians deliver our earliest—though by no means primitive—evidence of human thought. It is thus appropriate to characterize Egyptian thought as the beginning of philosophy. As far back as the third millennium B.C., the Egyptians were concerned with questions that return in later European philosophy and that remain unanswered even today—questions about being and nonbeing, about the meaning of death, about the nature of the cosmos and man, about the essence of time, about the basis of human society and the legitimation of power. Some of these questions will be explored here, in order to demonstrate that Egyptian answers, far from being primitive and antiquated, remain of interest today.

The Egyptians knew that their answers could not be definitive, and this flexible and pluralistic approach is the essence of their philosophical position. The idea that there is no single answer, that everything is flow and every answer provisional, is worth investigating today, in an age that has focused attention on fragmentation while continuing to cling to a history of absolutes. Without systematic and logical thought, the great achievements of ancient Egyptian culture are unthinkable. But Egyptian thought steers clear of monocausal simplification, convincing instead through refinement and association, through mastery of both word and image.

Egyptian thought is always pragmatic, like Egyptian teachings, which are oriented toward concrete life situations and renounce abstract ethical laws. Even Egyptian science, which saw its highest achievements in the areas of medicine and mathematics, was always directed to practical uses. For example, the Egyptians calculated time and created a calendar in the simplest and most practical way possible, even though this meant sacrificing astronomical exactness. Even the Egyptian notion of justice (*maat*) is characterized by its relationship to reality and human imperfection. The Egyptian emphasis on practical solutions is important to note, since reality cannot be mastered with intellect and abstract thought alone.

In Egyptian thought, extremes are avoided; measure and balance reign. The heart, not the brain, is the organ of thought. This distinction is relevant for modern psychology, which has begun to promote thinking with the heart. The refined view of man that we see in Egyptian anthropology, and the abundance of images in Egyptian religious thought—especially those in the Books of the Netherworld—have also received increased attention in modern psychology.

A study of ancient Egyptian thought brings us to the transition from prehistorical to historical time (around 3000 B.C.), when the first written records were kept and the first territorial state established.

The Egyptians were the earliest people to develop a literature and to erect monumental stone buildings. Despite these accomplishments, ancient misunderstandings and misinterpretations from the Greek and Roman periods have blocked our understanding of the Egypt of the pharaohs. Only with the development of Egyptology has a clearer reading of the Egyptian imagination developed. However, much work remains to be done before Egyptian ways of thinking are perhaps as familiar to us as those of Greece or medieval Europe.

This book is based on lectures delivered at the Eranos conference in Ascona (Ticino, Switzerland), where scholars from various disciplines have gathered annually since 1933 to acquaint themselves with the intellectual accomplishments of other cultures and to be stimulated by the many and varied forms of human thought.

Erik Hornung
Basel, 1992

CHAPTER I

W O R D

A N D

I M A G E

Hıeroglyphs, which first appeared in Egypt around 3000 B.C., were still being composed almost 3,500 years later. However, by the fifth century A.D. the initial meanings of the signs had become entirely obscured by fantastic allegorical interpretations. One of the last philosophers of the Alexandrian school, Horapollon, wrote a text on hieroglyphs in which he states: "When [the Egyptians] want to show 'open,' they paint a rabbit, for this animal always has its eyes open" (*Hieroglyphica*, I, 26); to indicate "mother" they paint a picture of a vulture, for as he points out, this species has no male; fertilization takes place through the wind (*Hieroglyphica*, I, 11). Horapollon was correct about the choice of signs for "mother" and "open," but he was quite wrong about the basis for choosing these hieroglyphs. The ancient Egyptians were far from such speculations; for them there were very simple phonetic connections between the image of a vulture and the word "mother," and between that of a hare and the verb "to open."

‹ Limestone "reserve" head from Giza, Dynasty 4,
circa 2450 B.C. Comprising only the head and
neck, the sculpture is complete. The Metropolitan
Museum of Art, New York.

After the fifth century A.D. the study and use of hieroglyphs ceased for approximately a thousand years. In 1419 a manuscript of Horapollon's *Hieroglyphica* was discovered on the Greek island of Andros. Only several years earlier, a translation by the Roman historian Ammianus Marcellinus of an Egyptian obelisk inscription had also resurfaced. Together, these two works became indispensable, authoritative sources of information for early Renaissance scholars attempting to interpret Egyptian hieroglyphs. They also inspired the invention of new visual symbols: in the fifteenth century Leone Battista Alberti and Antonio Averlino (known as Filarete) encouraged the use of such *lettere figurate* as decorative architectural elements, and countless fictive hieroglyphic inscriptions on imaginary ruins and monuments, complete with symbolic-allegorical translations, appeared in Francesco Colonna's illustrated book *Hypnerotomachia Polifili* (1499).

Numerous illustrations, imitations, and adaptations of Horapollon followed during the sixteenth century. Albrecht Dürer produced a series of illustrations for the *Hieroglyphica*; he also borrowed many of its symbols for his woodcut *Triumphal Arch* for the Emperor Maximilian. The purpose of this Renaissance picture-writing was to develop a universal language of visual images that scholars everywhere could understand and read. By the late sixteenth century, however, the new hieroglyphs had already begun to fall out of fashion. Rabelais and Johann Fischart, among others, mocked the "word twisters" who expressed abstract concepts by drawing objects whose names resembled the words for the intended concepts. By honoring the one-sided, purely symbolic interpretation of hieroglyphs, Renaissance scholars and artists hampered the later efforts of Athanasius Kircher in the seventeenth century, and others who followed him, to decipher Egyptian script, and thus promoted abstruse translations. Eighteenth-century attempts to understand hieroglyphs with the help of Chinese characters likewise met with failure, as the two writing systems and languages have fundamentally different structures.

Finally, in 1822, hieroglyphs were deciphered by Jean-François Champollion, who, aided by the trilingual inscriptions of the Rosetta Stone, understood that most of the signs were phonetic symbols. Champollion worked out the basic principles of the system with remarkable speed; only the signs for multiple consonants remained for his successor C. R. Lepsius to discover. Their work has enabled us to produce increasingly accurate readings of ancient Egyptian texts.

Our knowledge of the ancient Egyptian world of ideas is based on these written texts, along with visual images and archaeological finds. The sheer abundance of material that has survived is due in part to the favorable climate of the region, as well as to the tireless productivity of the ancient Egyptians. Most of the finds contain written texts or pictures, and very often a combination of the two, so word and image together provide a key to understanding ancient Egyptian sources.

The earlier written texts conveyed information that could not be understood through images alone. This information might be as straightforward as an economic report about a particular type of product, its origin, quality, or quantity. To register the delivery of "5 measures finest Libyan oil," for example, was a task for which the Egyptians needed something beyond a strictly pictorial language. But even more important than this type of information was the identification and preservation of the names of people and places the Egyptians represented in visual images. For themselves as well as for posterity the Egyptians wished to record which king had conquered and subjugated which lands. Their first records of historical events date to approximately the same time as their first notations about economic and administrative matters.

Writing was also important in connection with the affairs of the afterlife. The Egyptians believed that the dead person lived on in the hereafter, along with his name, which was inextricably linked with the essence of all that existed in the world. In the early dynasties, stelae were placed before burial mounds of kings and other members of the royal family. On these stone pillars only the name and title of the deceased were recorded. That the Egyptians used stone from the very beginning as a medium for writing is, of course, directly related to the desire to immortalize the person together with his or her name. Hieroglyphic writing in particular was designed to be chiseled into stone or painted on solid walls, that is, on permanent materials, while cursive hieratic writing was meant for papyrus or clay and was used only for keeping temporary records.

Some earlier Egyptologists believed that hieroglyphs grew out of an older, strictly pictorial writing system. A study by Kurt Sethe, published posthumously in 1939, announces this view in its title, *From Image to Letter* (*Vom Bilde zum Buchstaben*). Yet in the afterword to Sethe's own study, another scholar, Siegfried Schott, casts doubt on the thesis that a pictographic writing system predated Egyptian hieroglyphs. Several years after the publication of Sethe's work, Alexander Scharff produced additional archaeological evidence to support the newer thesis that the Egyptians actually invented writing at the beginning of historical time. Today this view has found general acceptance among scholars, some of whom think that writing might even have been the invention of a single person. This theory, in fact, is not new; it is proposed in Plato's *Phaedrus*, which introduces the inventor of writing in the character of Thoth, or Hermes Trismegistus.

In recent years a number of scholars have adopted the position that there were earlier stages in the development of the hieroglyphic system as we know it, that is, as it existed circa 3000 B.C. But in the absence of material evidence this theory remains questionable. If the Egyptians did have some pre- or proto-hieroglyphic writing system, some traces might well have survived in the exceptionally arid climate. However, we know of no such traces.

I am convinced that the ancient Egyptian system of writing represents an invention made around 3000 B.C. in order to express information that could not be conveyed by other means. From the very beginning writing has been a daughter of art. By 3000 B.C. the Egyptians had developed an extensive vocabulary in the visual arts that enabled them to represent such complex subjects as the hunt, the conquest of enemies, burials, even their hopes for the afterlife. To complement and extend this capability they needed a kind of writing that would allow them to do more than they could with a script based solely on pictures. They needed a writing system with a phonetic, rather than a pictographic, basis.

An artist could express the action of a king—smiting his enemy, preparing a building, celebrating a festival—but not his name. To write the king's name, additional pictures expressing sounds were needed; only the stable consonants mattered, not the fluctuating vowels. The famous commemorative Palette of Narmer, the first monumental work of Egyptian art, from shortly after 3000 B.C., is an excellent example. The palette illustrates the conquest of Lower Egypt and depicts the king, one arm raised, smiting the foe kneeling before him. That this is a representation of King Narmer is indicated by the images of a catfish and a chisel on both sides of the palette in the upper register. These images are used as phonograms and have nothing to do with the illustration of the battle and victory. The name and title of the participant indicate both the time and location of an event. This palette not only depicts the unification of Egypt under a single ruler, but it also marks the beginning of the written historical record of Egypt. Shortly afterward, at the beginning of Dynasty 1, King Aha intro-

Limestone funerary stela of King Djet, fourth
king of Dynasty 1, from Abydos. Musée du
Louvre. The bird represents the king as the
earthly incarnation of the falcon god Horus. It
stands on a rectangle designating the palace
floor within which is a representation of the
palace façade. The cobra is the hieroglyph *djet*
(snake). The entire composition may be read as
"the Horus Djet."

duced the names of years, so that historical information became more precise.

For several centuries hieroglyphic writing was used only on rare occasions. Nothing that we might call a continuous text appeared. At most we find a series of key words strung together, but not divided into sentences as such. Gradually in the Old Kingdom (2640–2134 B.C.) a kind of literature did develop. The Egyptians attributed the first proverbs (of which we have no written record) to Imhotep, a sage who lived in Dynasty 3 under King Djoser. An early stage in the development of writing exists in the inscriptions of tombs for Egyptian officials. These brief accounts of their position and influence during their lifetime are of particular importance in the history of writing. As Egyptologist Jan Assmann has aptly put it, for the Egyptians "the tomb is the preschool of literature."

At first the style of writing is noticeably economical: clear endings and phonetic aids to reading are rare, and verbs are often omitted altogether since there is always a visual representation of the event described. Further, hieroglyphs do not adhere to any single organizational scheme. Prior to the Old Kingdom they do not even occur in rows. A strong preference is shown, it is true, for writing from right to left, the direction characteristic of Hebrew and Arabic, but the Egyptians used other directions as well, in order to make allowances for pictures or particular architectural features. In symmetrical compositions hieroglyphs are oriented toward the middle axis—on the right side the signs run from left to right, on the left side they run the other way. When the king is shown celebrating before a god or goddess, the texts recited by both partners are oriented in the direction the figures face. Thus figures and text are composed as a unity, contrary to the Assyrian habit of writing cuneiform directly over the figures.

While the early inscriptions show limited means of expression, in another sense they are quite rich. They already contain both phonetic symbols and visual signs. When discussing the Egyptian writing system we usually distinguish between the following types of signs: ideograms or logograms, which are read as visual representations of specific objects; phonograms, signs that stand for single consonants or a series of two to three consonants (vowels are suggested only in foreign names); and determinatives, which indicate the category or type of word but are not themselves read. A single sign can belong to all three of these groups: the outline of a farmyard, as seen in the examples of hieroglyphs (1), can be read as the word *per* (house), but when used in the verb *peri* (to go out) the farmyard sign serves only as a phonetic symbol for the consonant string *p-r*. The same sign appears also in descriptions of buildings or parts of buildings, and in this context it functions as an identifying or classificatory sign which is not read but merely helps indicate the order of terms.

Like modern designers of information signs, the Egyptians always strove for clarity and simplicity when determining the shape of a sign, as the drawing of examples of hieroglyphs shows. For "tooth" they chose not the human tooth but the far more conspicuous elephant tusk (2); for "tongue" they used a snake's tongue (3); and for "ear" or "hearing," a cow's ear (4). Throat, thigh, and other body parts also appear in their animal form; the fore- and hindquarters of a lion stand for these parts on any animal. But the Egyptians chose human rather than animal shapes whenever the human body part itself had an easily identifiable shape; for instance, the head, eye, mouth, breast, arm, or leg. With internal organs it is often difficult to tell whether human or animal forms are depicted.

Whether representing body parts or other natural objects, the Egyptians tried to show the object from the most easily identifiable angle. Thus "eye" (5) and "mouth" (6) are expressed in frontal position,

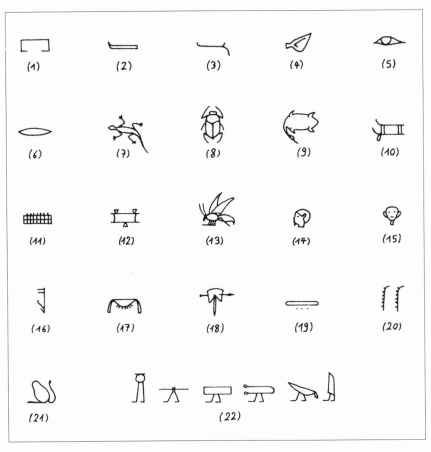

Examples of hieroglyphs.

mammals and birds in profile; the lizard (7), beetle (8), plucked goose (9), and other animals are shown from above. For purposes of clarity, the combination of perspectives was allowed: "transport sled" (10), like some pieces of furniture, combines side and overhead views, and "board game" (11) shows the board from above but the playing pieces from the side.

In some cases the inventors of hieroglyphs, faced with a wide variety of types, needed to find a single representative sign. For example, when trying to decide on a sign for "house," they disregarded all variants of existing house shapes and opted instead for the outline of a farmyard: a rectangular shape representing a brick wall with an opening on one side. Regardless of any changes in the actual construction of houses and temples, the same sign was used for millennia. In general, once the Egyptians settled on a particular sign they neither modernized it nor altered it in any other way.

However, it was not always possible on the first try to devise a definitive, sufficiently simple and clear shape for a particular sign. The sign for "path" is initially crooked, marked with footprints, and bordered by many bushes. Only later does it develop the simplified shape shown in example (12): the footprints disappear and the path becomes a pair of straight lines framed by three schematized bushes. In the Early Period, the bee (13) does not yet have the characteristic bipartite insect body, and many bird signs acquire clear, elegant outlines only in the course of time.

New signs were developed as new architectural forms appeared. The pyramid and obelisk, different forms of pillars, the pylon, or temple façade, and even such constructions as the stela and false door are all represented in the hieroglyphic system. New weapons, pieces of equipment, animals, and foreign peoples also find their way into the writing system. The Egyptians began to use the horse and wagon during the time that Asiatic rulers, the Hyksos, dominated Egypt (1650–1540 B.C.), and they incorporated signs for both into their writing system at the beginning of the New Kingdom. Later contact with foreigners likewise brought new signs into the ever-growing, never really completed system.

Unlike other writing systems, hieroglyphs assign color, or a combination of colors, to every sign; this tendency underscores the close relationship of Egyptian writing to the visual arts. Hieroglyphs are not pure graphemes; they are also pictures of reality, and as such they could reflect in some way the colors of the world they represent. Each sign in the system therefore has both a set shape and a particular color. The Egyptians used only red, yellow, green, blue, white, and black. They did not mix these colors to create new colors, nor did they pay attention to such nuances as the difference between light and dark shades. Plants and objects made of plant matter are always green in the hieroglyphic system, body parts and wooden objects red, the sky blue, and the earth black. In some cases the choice derives from an object's natural color; in others it does not. The color of many bird signs does not correspond to the bird's actual appearance; similarly, black is used for waves, blue for clay or clay bricks, and blue or green for the horns of hoofed animals.

Color can express something about the fundamental character of an object. The Egyptian language itself suggests this symbolic potential; the word for "color" can be used as a synonym for "essence" or "character." The red used in the written character for the "evil" bird (sparrow) has decidedly negative connotations. Red also evokes the association "blood," as when it is used with the sign for a butcher knife of stone or metal. Aside from its symbolic possibilities, coloration offers a practical way to differentiate between signs. Red distinguishes the sparrow from the swallow, for instance, since the outline of both birds is often identical. Coloration also helps distinguish between the two signs based on the shape of the male head. In the drawing of hieroglyphs, the sign showing the head in profile (14) is red, while the frontal head (15) is yellow. In this case, color has no symbolic value; it merely enables the Egyptians to use the same body part for two distinct characters.

In some cases simplicity in the shape and color of hieroglyphs pro-

Hieroglyphs from the Dynasty 18 tomb of
Haremheb, Valley of the Kings. The hieroglyphs
were first sketched in red and the final version of
the text, with corrections, was made in black.

duces limitations in the inventory of the signs. There are none to suggest the magnificence and variety of Egyptian gardens. Differences between individual flowers and fruits seem to have mattered little, and of the many fruits and vegetables known to the Egyptians, only the cucumber, fig, and wine grape appear as signs. Although they were familiar with a variety of different leaf shapes, they included only the lotus leaf in their writing system.

On the other hand, the hieroglyphic system contains a wide variety of bird signs. More than eighty different bird shapes were used, some of them among the most frequently occurring signs. The owl, for example, which has no great importance in the visual arts, appears quite often in writing, where it stands for the consonant *m* in the same way that a quail chick stands for the consonant *w*. These ubiquitous bird signs were such a distinctive feature of Egyptian writing that medieval Islamic authors referred to hieroglyphs in general as "bird writing." Ancient Egyptian scribes and stonemasons could not always tell the difference between similarly shaped bird signs; coloration often proved to be the only sure way to distinguish between them, and in some cases the surrounding context alone could help determine which particular bird sign was meant.

Unlike birds, mammals are relatively easy to distinguish from one another. Some of the animals that appear as signs were not indigenous to Egypt; these include the elephant, rhinoceros, giraffe, and baboon, which had been introduced from the Sudan or even more remote African regions. Notably, bears and deer, animals introduced from the Near East, were not rendered as signs in the writing system, although they did appear as motifs in Egyptian art.

As mentioned earlier, the Egyptians strove to give their signs not only individual, recognizable shapes but also particular phonetic values. A visual image often suffices to indicate a noun, but language comprises more than nouns; other parts of speech—adjectives, verbs, pronouns—prove difficult, even impossible, to express in a purely pictographic system.

First, a visual sign may become a phonetic symbol when the name of the depicted object sounds like another word; the word for the object is thus detached from its original, strictly visual meaning. For example, a rabbit (*wen*) becomes the sign for "to open" (*wen*), a farmyard (*per*) comes to represent the verb "to go out" (*peri*), and a star (*seba*) stands for "to teach" (*seba*). Vowels and endings of the words involved may differ; only the similarity of consonants matters.

Second, the desired word may appear as a combination of phonetic symbols, and in extreme cases may be written purely alphabetically. Here again, only consonants matter; variable vowels are ignored altogether. This second option quickly became a popular way to write the names of gods: "Ptah" occurs as *p* plus *t* plus *h*, "Sobek" as *s* plus *b* plus *ḳ*, "Amun" as *i* plus *mn* (a double-consonant sign) plus *n*. Especially in the Old Kingdom, the writing system reflects a concerted, at times even compulsive, effort to capture a series of sounds in several different ways: a triple-consonant sign might be followed and completed by three individual consonant signs; these signs, known as phonetic complements, play an important role in writing.

Third, a visual sign may be used metaphorically or metonymically to refer to a phonetically unrelated word. "Wind" or "gust" is indicated with the image of a sail, and "old" with that of a bowed man with a cane. "Bone" is denoted with a harpoon tip fashioned from bone (16), "gold" with a gilded collar (17), and "to shoot" with an animal skin pierced by an arrow (18). Such "idea signs" can be very abstract: a black hole indicates "death" or "enemy who has been destroyed"; a curved line expresses "crooked" in a moral sense; "hidden" is a blank space, a sign that cannot be seen.

In principle, any image might serve as a hieroglyph. The first inventors were wise enough to concentrate on a strictly limited number, but in discovering new applications of their invention and in composing longer texts for all purposes, a greater number of signs was needed. An increasing use was made of determinatives—signs that are not read but that determine the meaning of words. Thus in Middle and New Egyptian, walking legs are attached to every verb of motion, a skin to the name of every mammal, the sun to every expression of time, and so forth. This classification is helpful, as it allows words having the same consonants to be easily distinguished.

Even words written in a straightforward phonetic fashion become infused with symbolic meaning and help encode theological statements. The name of the god Ptah itself contains an allusion to his act of creation: the name is written to indicate heaven, earth, and the god dividing them, and it acquires an additional symbolic dimension when the scarab beetle replaces the sign for "earth" (19).

Egyptian writing contains a whole series of signs with more extensive, symbolic meanings related to their use as powerful talismans. Among these signs are the wounded eye of Horus or *udjat* eye, the life-span *ankh*, the scarab, and the *djed*, a pillar that derives its form from the bound sheaf of the first grain of the harvest. In an inscription we read *djed* as the verb "to endure," but in a visual composition it may have altogether different meanings. At times it refers to the god Osiris. *Djed* may also stand, like the *udjat* eye, for the complex myth of the wounding and healing of the eye of Horus that renews world order, or for the sun or moon; on occasion it refers to sacrifice or magical protection.

Whereas a written character should have a single, clear meaning, a symbol is essentially polysemic and complex; it stands for concepts and insights that individual words in a language can intimate but

Hieroglyphs from the Litany of Re, in the corridor
of the Dynasty 19 tomb of Siptah, Valley of the Kings.

Isis and Nephthys adoring the *djed* pillar, which is labeled "Osiris lord of *djed* [stability]." Exterior of the foot end of the box for the inner coffin of Nany, from Thebes, Dynasty 21. The Metropolitan Museum of Art, New York.

never fully capture. A symbol points toward something that in the end remains ineffable. Behind such symbols as *djed* or *udjat* stand entire myths, and although we may be able to relate a given myth in minute detail, we still never fathom its entire meaning.

The final phase of hieroglyphic writing, the system known as enigmatic writing or cryptography, plays with the symbolic value of signs. The earth-dwelling scarab beetle, for example, was used as a sign for "earth." Similarly, a lion, bull, or sphinx stands for "master," an egg for the concept "located within," a uraeus snake for "goddess," and a winged sun for "king." Enigmatic writing also employs complete pictures as verbal symbols. A king's title is composed of images of gods;

this "spelling" underscores the notion of the king's divinity. But despite their appearance these images are basically verbal in character. No additional written text accompanies them, and they occur in combination with ordinary hieroglyphs. A further step transforms such images into three-dimensional sculptural groups intended to be read as the name of a king.

The Egyptian system of writing, the representation of deities, and signs including *ankh*, *djed*, and *udjat*, which appear both in and out of writing as symbols and talismans, all help realize the expressive potential of the visual image. Ultimately the Egyptians used the power of the image as a means of describing and constructing their world in a way that went well beyond the possibilities offered by the written word alone. In New Kingdom temples, triumphal images of the pharaoh's victory over all enemies decorated the exterior walls and entrance towers. Intended to ward off evil spirits from the sacred area of the temple, these images were not so much descriptions of specific events as stylized motifs. Like the image of the sun's movement or the unification of the Two Lands, the motif of the defeat of the enemies used in Egyptian temples is more complex than an individual symbol. It connotes a general, even universal truth about the way of the world. After the Amarna Period, in the fourteenth century B.C., however, this generalized form of representation gave way to more or less realistic depictions of specific battle scenes. Sety I decorated the north wall of the Great Pillared Hall at Karnak with scenes of his campaigns in the Near East and his successful return to Egypt. Ramesses II repeatedly depicted episodes from the battle of Kadesh on his temples, and thereby developed the images into what Jan Assmann describes as "a propaganda campaign of heretofore unknown magnitude." The battle appears with accompanying written text a total of ten times in the temples of Abydos, Abu Simbel, Luxor, and Thebes–West; we also have literary accounts of it written on papyrus.

The battle of Kadesh took place in 1274 B.C., the fifth year of Ramesses II's reign. Waged against the Hittites and their allies, it was by no means an Egyptian victory: the Egyptian reconnaissance failed, and Ramesses was barely able to escape from a trap set by his enemies on the Orontes. Only his personal intervention and the well-timed arrival of fresh troops enabled the Egyptian army to manage an organized retreat. Although neither side could actually claim victory at Kadesh, this particular confrontation marked a turning point in the ongoing hostilities between the Egyptians and the Hittites. After several further battles, the two powers began negotiations that led to a formal peace agreement in the twenty-first year of Ramesses' reign, and to an alliance through marriage thirteen years later. The battle scenes are not so much triumphal images of a pharaoh as testimony to a policy that eventually brought about peace.

One scene, which is consistently overlooked in discussions of Ramesses' determination to enforce his peace policy, is particularly striking. The scene in question is depicted on the western exterior wall of the Luxor temple, facing the Nile. It is at the end of a series of battle scenes, and it presents a completely ravaged landscape: A destroyed city on a hill is visible to the right, its gates open and overturned, its brick walls crumbling in decay. A desolate area containing only felled or uprooted trees and bushes extends to the left. No stirring of life is seen; even the enemy dead, usually shown in chaotic Egyptian battle scenes, are absent. The utter barrenness becomes even more striking when compared with the normal scenes of occupation and conquest favored by Ramesses in other temples, where the vivid activity of battle overshadows the impression of death and destruction. The scene has an undeniably strong impact on viewers even thousands of years later and needs no special explanation. It shows the absolutely devastating consequences of war with shocking clarity. Unlike other Egyptian battle scenes, there is no accompanying written text to provide information not readily available in the visual images; complete anonymity is its aim. The relentless destruction effaces even the names of the particular site and the demolished city. The depiction utterly transcends its particular context and reflects a timeless, universal truth through a visual image that goes far beyond the possibility of a verbal message—as is, after all, the purpose of art.

CHAPTER 2

O R I G I N S

Myths of creation have a fundamental, exemplary importance in every culture: only the recollection of an ideal, perfect beginning of the world and of human existence enables us to overcome crises and begin anew. The Egyptian phrase *sep tepi* (the first time), used in reference to creation, evokes the magic that radiates from every beginning, every first time. The ancient Egyptian designation shows that creation was perceived not as a single, isolated event, but instead as something that entailed constant repetition. In the Egyptians' view, the world could become repeatedly as new and perfect as at the time of its origin. From this conviction they drew much of the creative power that continues to impress us today.

If we consult written texts and visual images for specific, direct statements about the creation of the world, we may be disappointed at first; no Egyptian account of creation comparable to the Hebrew Book of Genesis or the Babylonian Enuma Elish exists until the Ptolemaic and Roman periods (fourth century B.C. and later), when we find detailed, coherent descriptions of Egyptian cosmogony in temple texts. From the earlier Pharaonic Period we have only isolated statements and a wealth of allusions from different centuries and completely different types of texts, as well as depictions of individual events, most notably the separation of earth and sky.

‹ Statue of an unnamed official from a Dynasty 5
tomb at Giza. The Metropolitan Museum of Art,
New York.

Taken together, these statements and images nonetheless yield a refined picture of creation. The Egyptians knew that the event of creation could not be grasped by means of a single, simple formulaic principle. They recognized the need to find ever new ways and symbols to express ideas that were essentially inexpressible. In one version of the myth the creator uses his seed, in another version language, and in still another his hands, but in each case the central question remains the same: How could being issue from nonbeing, and the many from the one?

Believing first of all that the world had a beginning, the Egyptians concluded that the world must also have both spatial and temporal limits, even if such limits remained indistinct and were conceived of only in very general terms as being millions of years and miles away. Modern cosmogony has refined rather than replaced this early insight. Measurements and calculations have helped determine the spatial and temporal horizons of our world with increased precision, but those horizons still are not entirely comprehensible to us.

The Egyptians formulated ideas about conditions prior to creation and beyond the created world. Such notions occur particularly often in texts of the Ptolemaic and Roman periods, but they extend back as far as the Pyramid Texts from the Old Kingdom. According to these accounts, the world emerges from a primeval darkness (*keku semau*) and a primeval flood (*nun*) that are indistinguishable from one another. Blended together, darkness and flood represent all that was prior to creation.

The Egyptians often described the primeval state in negative terms. To them it was the negation of all the world's distinguishing features, and they even had a special grammatical form indicating "when . . . did not yet exist." Neither gods nor humans had come into being yet, and heaven and earth (including the underworld, *dat*), like day and night, rested undivided in a darkness that knew neither time nor space. Because there was no life, there was also no death. No name had been given, no form and no thing created. The phrase from the Pyramid Texts of the Old Kingdom "when strife did not yet exist" negates not only the mythical conflict between Horus and his brother Seth, but every form of conflict in this inert, undifferentiated state. In the Coffin Texts, from about 2000 B.C., the condition is described as the time "when two things did not yet even exist."

The creator drifts in this primeval morass without finding a fast hold. But gradually the mud of the primordial flood becomes a single mass and rises as a hill—an image that the Egyptians had before their eyes every autumn, when the annual Nile floods receded. Firm ground separates itself from the watery mass; the creator can stand on such ground, and his work can begin. The One gives way to four pairs of primordial creatures, the Ogdoad, whose names indicate that they belong to the realm of the uncreated: primeval flood, hiddenness, endlessness, the undifferentiated ones. The sun emerges from the center of these beings, and as it rises for the first time it signals the beginning of the world.

The motif of emergence, associated with the image of a mound of earth, is reflected in the pyramids. Another equally popular, albeit later, symbol of emergence is the lotus flower that grows out of the muddy depths. Being springs from its blossom, once again taking the form of the sun. The image of the "sun god on the blossom" originates after the Amarna Period around 1350 B.C. It occurs most often as a ram-headed god on a primeval lotus, and occasionally as a sun child atop a lotus bud. Another apparently quite old image of emergence is that of a mighty cow rising out of the originating waters, bearing the sun between its horns. In the Old Kingdom Pyramid Texts, this cow is identified as Mehetweret, or "Great Swimmer," and later also as Ihet

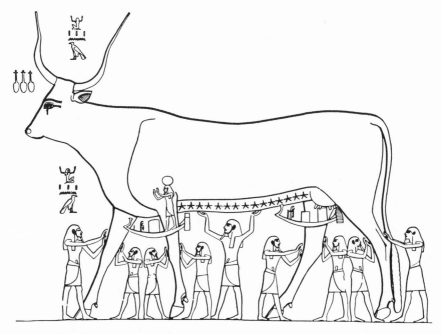

The celestial cow on the outermost shrine of
Tutankhamun.

or Ahet, and it appears in manifestations of such goddesses as Hathor
and Neith. The celestial cow is seen already at the end of prehistoric
times, in the form of a cow's head adorned with stars; from the Coffin
Texts on, the celestial cow also represents the mother of the sun god,
Re, who gives birth to him anew each day. The images of primeval hill,
lotus, and cow provide a visual approximation or paraphrase for the
notion of a foundation that is integral to the Egyptian concept of creation.

The sun rises out of this foundation and creates space with its light
and time with its daily path across the sky. One of the Egyptian incarnations of the creator god is a bird whose shriek pierced the original
stillness before the sun emerged from the bird's egg, the primeval seed

of the world (Leiden Hymn to Amun, 80). This same bird may also be interpreted as the heron Benu, the first living creature to settle on the earth mound, and one that appears in the classical tradition as the phoenix. The creator can assume many different shapes besides that of a bird; he can be a human being or, quite often, a snake, the most primeval creature.

In human form, the creator appears as Atum, "the undifferentiated one," who either produces the first sperm by masturbating or generates the first divine couple by spitting or coughing them out. Like the biblical Adam and Eve, this first sexually differentiated couple, Shu and Tefnut, must necessarily come into being without copulation; as the Coffin Texts specifically state, Shu "was not formed in an egg." Natural procreation begins with this pair, whose own children are Geb and Nut. Atum and these four, along with the four gods of the following generation (Osiris, Isis, Seth, and Nephthys), make up the ninefold system that plays such an important role in Egyptian theology. Although there are frequent references to this ennead and the attendant cosmogony as "Heliopolitan," it should be noted that actually they stand independent of Heliopolis, and any other specific time or place.

The Egyptians liked to juxtapose the concept of an ennead with that of a cosmogony in which Ptah or Ptah-Tatenen figures as the creator. In contrast to Atum, Ptah creates with language: having first devised the world in his heart, he then calls it into existence with his tongue. Our main source of information about this constellation of ideas is the so-called Monument of Memphite Theology, now in the British Museum in London, which was copied onto stone in 700 B.C. ostensibly from an earlier worm-eaten text. Egyptologists were long inclined to believe that the monument dated back at least to the Old Kingdom. Further research has revealed that in fact it should be dated later than the Amarna Period and Akhenaton's revolution (after 1325 B.C.), when Memphis and the god Ptah played more prominent roles.

Creation through the word is by no means associated with Ptah alone. As an independent concept it occurs as early as the Pyramid Texts. The sun god, for example, makes use of insightful planning (Sia), creative statement (Hu), and powerful magic (Heka). These three creative powers accompany him on his nocturnal journey through the Netherworld, and help him renew his creative work. According to other sources, the goddess Neith called the world into being through seven statements, which in a later magic text become the sevenfold laugh of the creator god. In the figure of Neith we confront a demiurge who represents more than a late, localized development. Although we get a clearer understanding of this cosmogony only in later texts from Sais and Esna, where Neith had particular centers of worship, her close ties to the primeval cow Mehetweret link her with the early image of the celestial cow. If we consider Neith's important role in the Early Period, and her early incarnation as a beetle, we see that while she holds a central position in early cosmogonic conceptions, these are later eclipsed by others. The beetle Neith disappears, for instance, and gives way to the dung beetle of the sun god, the scarab Khepri.

In addition to worshipping Neith, the Egyptians in Esna honored Khnum as a creator god. With the power of his hands he forms human beings, and also the primeval egg together with the world, on a potter's wheel. Ptah also represents this kind of creator. The god of artists and artisans, he not only calls forth the world through language but forms it as his personal handiwork.

It is impossible to organize the above-mentioned notions of creation and creators in terms of some temporal or geographical scheme. The complex phenomenon of the world's beginning is presented in so many diverse ways that individual ideas and images intermingle and supplement each other. In the Late Period, for example, each temple had its own preferred cosmogony, yet it was still permissible to worship other creator gods and their work in the same temple.

Neither the creator god's persona nor the mode of creation is rigidly fixed, but different accounts of the god reveal a number of shared attributes. Whatever the creator's individual character, it is always the god who "came into being by himself" (*kheper djesef*); without parents, this god "formed his egg himself" (Leiden Hymn to Amun, 100). Further, the god predates the division into male and female; it is both male and female, father and mother. Above all, the creator god is the one who initially stands alone, but then makes "himself into millions," according to a description dating from after the Amarna Period. The designation has many precursors. The early ninefold system that derives from Atum, for example, suggests just this kind of development, whereby the one becomes the many. For the Egyptians the number nine as the intensified plural (three times three) expresses an all-encompassing totality. The Middle Kingdom Coffin Texts (II, 39) contain a statement that is considered the earliest reference to the notion of a trinity. The statement concerns the time when the god Atum "gave birth to Shu and Tefnut in Heliopolis, when he was one and became three." In the simplest of terms, this expresses the notion that from unity comes diversity.

In sum, the monotheism of the Egyptians consists in the belief that in the beginning the divine was one, and that in the cosmogony that was the work of the one, the one became many. In austere monotheistic fashion, the Egyptians emphasize the privileged status of the original one in always new—and often paradoxical—descriptions and epithets for the creator god. According to a New Kingdom hymn to the sun alluding to Atum's having produced the first seed with his own hand, he is "the one who begat his begetter, who engendered his mother, who created his own hand" (Assmann, *Ägyptische Hymnen und Gebete*, hymn no. 51). As the One, Atum still belongs to the realm of nonbeing; through his transformation into the first divine couple, he enters being. Yet in the Monument of Memphite Theology mentioned above it is the god Ptah who enjoys priority. Called the "father of Atum," he is the creator of the one who himself has no creator, and his name Ptah-Nun signals that he also contains Nun, the flood of water before creation, in his being.

The work of creation is nothing more than the separation and differentiation of the world from the one of beginning. The Egyptians described this event in numerical terms with the formula: The one becomes the many, what is singular becomes plural. They gave visual expression to this notion in an image depicting the separation of the earth from the sky. In this image Atum's son Shu separates the celestial

The air god Shu holding up the sky goddess Nut, with the earth god Geb reclining below. Exterior of the inner coffin of Nany, Thebes, Dynasty 21. The Metropolitan Museum of Art, New York.

goddess Nut from the earth god Geb. In the system of the ennead, Nut and Geb are Shu's children, and the parents of Osiris and Isis. The Pyramid Texts and Coffin Texts refer to the event of separation, but it occurs as a visual image only at the end of the New Kingdom and is found primarily in papyrus scrolls and on sarcophagi of Dynasty 21. Shu's elevation of the sky completes the work of creation begun by Atum. It delimits the structured world from what is still formless, and creates space.

Creatures of all kinds gradually populate the earth. The Egyptians did not single out the creation of human beings in particular. For the most part human beings are mentioned together with gods as the handiwork of the primeval creator god. Humans are said to have sprung from the creator's tears; the words for "tear" and "human" in Egyptian are similar. But the explanation is more than a play on words. It also reflects the ambivalent origins of humanity in a temporary blurring of the god's vision. In the Coffin Texts the creator asserts that "humans belong to the blindness behind me" (VI, 344); the statement intimates why humans are so often struck blind. While human beings originate in the creator's tears, the gods issue from the same god's sweat. Consequently, the sweat associated with the Egyptian gods carries a sweet smell; the odor envelops them in an aura that always betrays their presence.

In the beginning, gods and humans inhabit the earth under the rule of a divine dynasty that precedes the historical kings. At its apex stands Re, the sun god, lord of all creatures. Human beings can bask in the constant presence of the sun during this early period; there is no change from day to night, nor does the underworld exist. It is the Golden Age, the blessed time (*pa'ut*) in which *maat*, or proper, harmonious order, comes to human beings and directs their lives.

The Book of the Celestial Cow describes how this ideal initial phase of existence eventually came to an end, superseded by the decidedly unidyllic current way of life. The reason for the change lies in the aging process that affects all living things. The youthful freshness of creation eventually fades, and the sun grows old; darkness, in contrast, can never age. Written in the fourteenth century B.C., during the Amarna Period, the Book of the Celestial Cow describes the sun god as an aged man whose grip on the reins of power gradually slackens. Even the Egyptian gods are subject to the aging process of the mortal world; not even they enjoy the privilege of eternal life.

As the strength of the sun god wanes, oppositional forces come into play. Humans devise attacks against Re and must be punished. Some meet destruction through the god's fiery eye, but as in myths of the great flood, others survive and repopulate the earth. The sun retreats from the earth on the back of the celestial cow, and darkness reigns for the first time since creation; in their blindness, surviving human beings turn against one another, distancing themselves from the gods forever. The other gods retreat with the sun god into the heavens, and Osiris acquires dominion over the newly created underworld. The inevitable consequence of aging is death, which brings even the life and power of the gods to an end; Shu follows his father the sun god and Re's appointed representative, the moon god Thoth; Horus becomes the heir of Osiris.

Henceforth war and violence shape the lives of human beings. Having lost the paradisiacal innocence of their beginnings, they can regain access to the world of the gods only in death. Moreover, their rebellion suggests a dangerous threat to the continued existence of creation itself, insofar as it hints at the existence of destructive forces that seek to bring the normal course of events on earth to a halt. The dragon of chaos known as Apophis embodies this danger. The threat of total dissolution finds expression also in the Egyptians' anxiety that the sky could fall to earth. Should space collapse in this way, it would effect a return to the original state in which all was one. The Egyptian sorcerer who invokes such a collapse to strengthen his spells utters the most terrible threat imaginable. The Book of the Celestial Cow describes in detail the tremendous effort involved in keeping the sky supported; the most important element of this effort is time.

At the end of time, sky and earth will be reunited and the sun will cease to mark the visual pulse of the world. Primeval waters and darkness will fill the cosmos once again, and only the creator will survive. In the form of a snake, he will return to the chaos from which he once emerged. Such reflections on eschatology occur only rarely in Egyptian texts, but they do exist, and their presence contributes to the symmetry of beginning and end that characterizes the Egyptian conception of the world.

Creation carries within itself the seeds of decay, and it is only through aging and decline that regeneration and rejuvenation can take place. This fundamental idea of Egyptian culture helps explain many of that civilization's creative powers and accomplishments. As we have seen, creation is not a single, completed occurrence, in the Egyptian view; it is in need of continual repetition and confirmation. Form can be defined only against that which is formless; and regeneration cannot occur without a journey through nonbeing. Prior to creation, chaos must rule once more.

Egyptian art contains many symbols of the idea of regeneration; two of the best known are the *udjat*, the wounded and healed eye of Horus, and the dung beetle or scarab that emerges repeatedly out of the earth. The dual image of threat and constant renewal finds expression also in the image of the ouroboros, the snake that bites its own tail. Surrounding the world with its gigantic body, the snake forms a complete circle that both protects and challenges existence on all sides. The

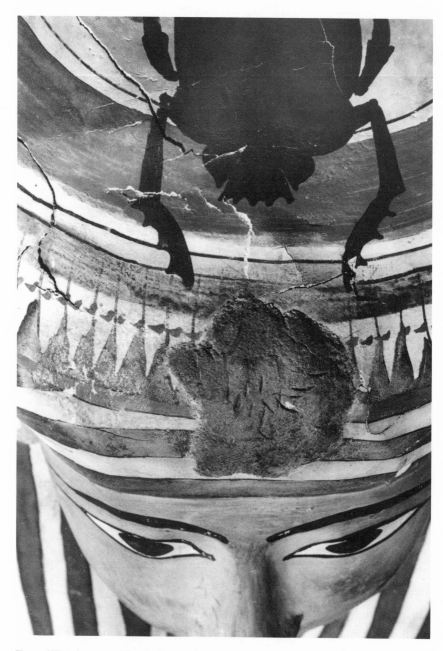

The god Khepri as a scarab beetle, the morning
manifestation of the sun god. Inner coffin of
Tabakenkhonsu, Dynasty 25. The Metropolitan
Museum of Art, New York.

ouroboros, found for the first time on a golden shrine of Tutankhamun from the Amarna Period, became known far beyond the borders of ancient Egypt. Modern physics could use the sign as a hieroglyph for the notion of a temporal-spatial continuum, and thereby recall one particular occurrence of the image that includes all of Egyptian ontology.

The image of an ouroboros is found on a coffin painting from Dynasty 21. The ouroboros surrounds a rabbit, the Egyptian written sign for *wen* (being). The rabbit appears on a standard otherwise reserved for images of the gods. Words can only approximate what this single image expresses so beautifully: divine being is enclosed by nonbeing, representing the world's horizons. Nonbeing is the space in which being continually renews itself, and is also the locus of the dissolution of being at the end of time. The nocturnal regeneration of being takes place in the body of the snake. In the New Kingdom text of the Amduat, the hour-by-hour account of the nightly voyage of the sun god through the Netherworld, we read that this process takes place inside "the encircler of the world"; the word thus anticipates the image.

For the Egyptians, creation repeats itself with every sunrise; this daily event represents the emergence of the creator god and returns youthful vigor to the world. The sun's light is the active, creative principle that gives shape to the world and renews it constantly. Akhenaton drew on this concept when he transformed the metaphorical description of the creator god as "the individual one with many hands" into a visual symbol of the divine solar disk, Aton, whose rays end in hands that grant life and protection to the king and royal family. But in his hymns of praise, Akhenaton concentrated too much on this image of the beneficent sun. He refused to accept that darkness too deserves praise, and his work foundered on that refusal. Traditional Egyptian hymns to the sun do not exclude the nocturnal side of life;

Rabbit on a standard, encircled by the ouroboros.
Drawing of a Dynasty 21 sarcophagus in the
Cairo Museum.

they depict the sun's descent into the Realm of the Dead as well, for
only this journey through the world's depths makes the morning renewal possible.

Aside from the sunrise, the beginning of the new year revises the
world and repeats creation. The Egyptians called the year "that which
rejuvenates itself" (*renpet*). On every New Year's Day it starts again,
and after a small beginning it increases in size. New Year's Day marks
both the birthday of the sun god and "the beginning of time"; in short,
it signals the return of creation.

Akhenaton and his family touched by the rays of the solar disk Aton, in a rock tomb at Tell el-Armana.

The renewal of creation occurs also in larger cycles through the person of the pharaoh. A new age was said to begin when each new pharaoh took the throne; Ramesses II indicates as much with the statement that he "grounded the world anew, as in creation." In accordance with the will of Tuthmosis III, Egypt should be "as if Re were its king," that is, as in the distant, idyllic time when gods still ruled the earth. To meet the demand for continual regeneration of existence, the rulers established rejuvenation festivals. After a thirty-year period or generation of rule, the king had ostensibly aged enough that a new king, or at least a renewed one, was needed to secure the world's continued existence. The old king was buried in the form of a statue, and as shown in images from Dynasty 18 onward, the *sed* festival following the ritual burial imbued him with youthful vitality and thus enabled him to continue to bear the burden of the world and support the heavens. The Egyptians celebrated the renewal of creation in a particularly ceremonious way when they founded a new temple. In their eyes, such an event brought an entire cosmos into being and established a new residence for the gods on earth. Whether in the daily sunrise or in the pharaoh's deeds, at the beginning of a new year or a new king's reign, the Egyptians felt the breath of the creator god upon them and experienced the living renewal of his work; hence their confidence to make pronouncements about the beginning of the world, a beginning that we can never really know.

CHAPTER 3

T I M E

A N D

E T E R N I T Y

Our ideas about time are rooted in ancient
Egypt: it was there that the system of the solar year now used throughout the Western world originated. The solar year, twelve months of
equal length and five additional, intercalary days, was ingeniously
simple. Because the solar year made no provision for a "leap day," there
was a discrepancy of approximately one fourth of a day vis-à-vis the
true, astronomical year. The Egyptians favored the solar year for its
clear organization and used it from the beginning of historical time.
While the early Egyptian calendar contained no leap day or leap year,
the concept of the latter also was developed in Egypt. The notion of
adding a day to the calendar every four years is usually associated with
the later Julian calendar, yet it was actually the Alexandrian calendar
of the Ptolemaic Period that served as a model.

Like the Egyptian year, the Egyptian month was organized sche-
matically and consistently, and divided into three ten-day periods. A

‹ Limestone sculpture of a bound Libyan, probably
from a royal funerary temple at Saqqara, Dynasty 5,
2400 B.C. The Metropolitan Museum of Art, New York.

lunar calendar corresponding to the true length of the month had existed since ancient times, but the Egyptians used it solely for religious purposes and consulted it primarily to help determine the dates of festivals. The current calendar, with months of different lengths and a seven-day week, may be—and has been—seen as unnecessarily complicated. In fact, the calendar reform of the French Revolution returned to the ancient Egyptian scheme—months of equal length, divided into three periods of ten days each. This reform, however, was short-lived.

The ancient Egyptians divided the day into twenty-four hours, twelve each for day and night. The individual hours were not all the same length originally; they varied in accordance with the seasons. The Egyptians did not subdivide the hour further into minutes and seconds. The shortest period of time, referred to as *at*, was a moment, but one of no specific length relative to the hour.

Together, hours, days, months, and years form the lifetime of a human being. The ancient Egyptians called this lifetime *aha'u* and in many instances measured it with utmost care. We have a wealth of information from the time of the pharaohs and the later Ptolemaic and Roman periods about age, and not only about the ages attained by people. The ages of the sacred bulls Apis and Buchis were likewise calculated meticulously and recorded on stone monuments. With the help of funerary stelae and mummy tablets from some of the larger funerary complexes it has even been possible to gather data about the average life span of the Egyptians, which—as a result of the high infant and childhood mortality rate—lay between twenty-five and thirty-three years. A generation lasted thirty years; this corresponds to the period celebrated by the *sed* festival, the festival of renewal held to rejuvenate the king thirty years after the beginning of his reign. Whoever survived the particularly threatening decades of early life had a good chance of living to a ripe old age. Several pharaohs reigned for more than fifty years, for example. As confirmed by contemporary monuments and the burial finds of his mummy, Ramesses II died in his sixty-seventh year on the throne, and although it cannot be proven with the same degree of accuracy, Pepy II, who ruled at the end of Dynasty 6, ostensibly reigned for ninety-four years.

Not only pharaohs but also officials sometimes carefully recorded information about their age. Netjeruhotep, a ship's manager, reported that as "a man of seventy-three years" he had led a desert expedition to the alabaster quarries of Hatnub—an extraordinary feat, to be sure, and for this reason recorded there for eternity. A statue (now in Munich) of Bakenkhons, the high priest of Amun under the aged Ramesses II, even lists the duration of individual phases of his life and his career; in total they add up to eighty-five years. In Dynasty 22, a priest of Amun named Nebnetjeru claimed to have reached the remarkable age of ninety-six, "healthy, without illness." He wrote further on a block statue (now in Cairo) that "if one desires the extent of my lifetime, one must implore God." The same age of ninety-six occurs on a mummy tablet from the Roman Period, and an even more advanced age, ninety-nine, supposedly was reached by the priest Besmut, who died in Dynasty 26 during the reign of Amasis. An inscription found in a Meir rock tomb and dating from the end of the Old Kingdom states that the priest of Hathor buried there "spent a lifetime up to one hundred years," but it remains an open question whether this assertion contains an exact figure, a convenient round number, or an idealized wish.

"One hundred years" was in any event the limit virtually no one surpassed. People might, however, express a desire for a longer life, well beyond this age. On a statue from Karnak, of Amenophis, a wise man later revered as a god, we read: "I have reached eighty years in that my favor with the king [Amenophis III] is great, and I will complete yet 110 years." The aforementioned high priest Bakenkhons makes the following wish to the god Amun: "May he grant me a lifetime in perfection, after 110 years."

For the Egyptians, "110 years" signifies the ideal limit of earthly existence. It is the age that occurs repeatedly in inscriptions, expressed in the form of a wish. The Old Testament likewise adopts this perfect age for Joseph and Joshua, and it appears also in the Gothic chronicle of Jordanis, where King Ermanarich is said to be 110 years old. This same round number corresponds more or less to the highest proven age reached by humans in more recent times.

In the Middle Kingdom Coffin Texts we read: "Each person familiar with this text will complete 110 years of life, of which ten years will be outside his inadequacy and his impurity, outside his offenses and his insincerity, as in the case of a man who was unknowing and became knowing." In other words, the Egyptians conceived of the ideal age as consisting of one hundred plus ten years, the ten-year period a bonus or gift—pure, unspoiled time beyond the round oldest age. The extra decade gave even the oldest person imaginable the chance to attain wisdom and freedom from all earthly shortcomings before that inevitable descent into the Realm of the Dead.

Some Egyptians, not content with the additional ten years, stretched it to twenty. In the tomb of Nebwenenef, a high priest of Osiris under Ramesses II, we find the wish: "You live 100 years and 20 years thereafter. This is my daily request of Re." This new ideal age of 120 years occurs in several Theban tombs of the Late Period, and again in the Old Testament, where we read that Moses surpassed Joseph and Joshua and reached the truly exceptional age of 120 years. Formulated here as a specific wish for ten or twenty years is the more general desire for more time, time that should be granted even a centenarian, since the human desire for time is limitless. Never satisfied, we always yearn for something beyond that lifetime determined by the gods or fate.

In a well-known travel report from the eleventh century B.C., the messenger Wenamun advises the prince of Byblos to erect a stone monument in his honor rather than make his mission more difficult. On this monument the following should be inscribed: "Amun-Re, King of the Gods, has sent me . . . his messenger in connection with the lumber for the large, glorious bark of Amun-Re, King of the Gods. I have felled the wood and loaded it; I have equipped him [the messenger] with my ships and my men, and I have let them proceed to Egypt in order to request of Amun fifty years of life beyond that which is my due." Such a wish was not unusual for an Egyptian, who knew that Amun could grant such requests since

> He saves whomever he chooses, even if he is in the underworld . . .
> He lengthens lifetime and subtracts from it,
> He grants an extension to the one he loves.

This particular version of the request occurs in the seventieth song of the Leiden Hymn to Amun. Another version occurs in spell 71 of the Book of the Dead:

> May you deliver me to the life that is in your hand.
> May [you] grant many years beyond the years of my life,
> Many months beyond the months of my life,
> Many days beyond the days of my life,
> Many nights beyond the nights of my life,
> Until I shall . . . go forth.

Notably, the very generally formulated plea for additional time on earth is addressed to the powers of fate in the Realm of the Dead. The request is not misdirected: one may receive more time in this life only

Mummies in their shrines, protected by a snake,
from the ninth hour of the Book of Gates in the
tomb of Haremheb, Valley of the Kings.

from sources in the afterlife. The recently published Vandier Papyrus
tells of a magician who descends into the Netherworld to request
more time for the ruling king. He is told that what he asks can be
granted, but on one condition: he, the magician, must offer himself in
place of the king and die.

In the Instruction of King Merikare from the First Intermediate
Period, humans are directed not to trust in the "length of years" since
the judges of the dead "see lifetime as a single hour." Captured here in
a metaphor, the relativity of time is illustrated even more clearly in the
Books of the Netherworld from the New Kingdom. These depict the
sun god on his nocturnal journey through the Realm of the Dead,

where he stays only an hour in each individual province of the underworld. A single hour in the afterlife corresponds to an entire lifetime on earth, and during this time the dead are awakened by the creative word of the god. They arise from their biers, accept clothes, food offerings, and other necessities of life, and are able to use their feet and other limbs. The deceased can view the god's majesty and even converse with him during this time. But as the sun god moves on to the next region at the end of the hour, they sink back into the sleep of death, their lifetime having come to an end once again.

This lifetime, continually renewed as the sun god travels through the underworld, is depicted in an illustration from the Book of Gates: twelve gods "carrying the lifetime in the west," the Realm of the Dead. The lifetime assumes the shape of a gigantic snake inscribed with the hieroglyphs for "lifetime." In this scene the inexhaustible supply of

An endlessly wound snake, representing the infinity of time, from the fourth hour of the Book of Gates in the tomb of Sety I, Valley of the Kings.

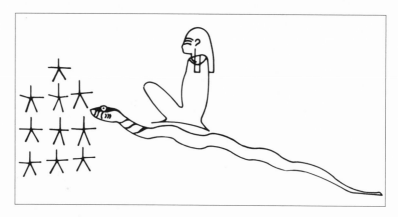

The serpent as an incarnation of time swallows the stars, the already expended hours of the night, from the eleventh hour of the Amduat in the Dynasty 18 tomb of Amenophis II, Valley of the Kings.

time offered by the afterlife is illustrated clearly. The blessed dead partake of it, and at the same time the wicked are destroyed. As enemies of the sun god they receive no portion of this time.

In the inscription accompanying the illustration the time snake is called *metui*, or "double cord." The expression refers to another scene in the Book of Gates in which time appears as a doubly twisted rope spun from the mouth of a deity. Stars above the twists in the rope mark the individual hours as measurable units of time. In this image both the beginning and the passage of time are expressed. Emerging from the hidden, divine depths of creation, time develops in a continuum with a clear structural organization and no gaps, and eventually falls back into the depths from which it first emerged. Each hour is born and devoured by the entirety of time, whose limit is eternity.

The Egyptian concept of eternity brings us to two important terms, *neheh* and *djet*. While the two terms do not signify eternity in an absolute sense, they do come as close as possible to meaning "eternity" without actually being synonymous with it, since they represent the sum of all conceivable units of time. However, unlike the notions of a primeval flood and darkness, *neheh* and *djet* never refer to regions outside creation. This Egyptian "eternity" has both a beginning and an end, and it consists of years and days. Thus it may be less misleading to speak of "time" than "eternity" when working in translation. In the Chonsumes Papyrus (now in Vienna), which dates from Dynasty 21, *neheh* and *djet* are joined by the "million years" as personifications of time, and the expression "million years" often occurs in written texts as a synonym for both of the other terms.

In the "Cannibal Hymn" of the Pyramid Texts (274), "the lifetime of Unas is *neheh*, his limit is *djet*." Unas was the last king of Dynasty 5, but the name might be replaced by that of any other pharaoh or, later, of anyone who had died. The same basic point is formulated even more succinctly in the Instruction of King Merikare: "Being there [existence in the afterlife] is *neheh*." The duration of existence in the afterlife is *neheh* and *djet*. In comparison, the duration of earthly existence is hardly worth consideration. This holds true for the Egyptian gods as well, since they are creatures of the beyond. It applies particularly to Re and Osiris, the lord of the underworld, often characterized by such epithets as "master of *neheh*" and "ruler of *djet*." According to the Book of the Dead, Osiris "lives a lifetime of millions of years" (spell 175). Each person becomes an Osiris after death, and as

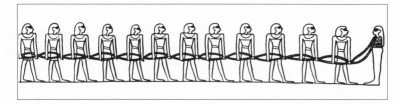

Time as an endless rope, from the Book of Gates
in the tomb of Ramesses VI, Valley of the Kings.

a result the hope for "millions of years"—which suggests something of the duration of *neheh* and *djet*—is not the privilege of the god alone, but extends to include all humanity.

With the concepts *neheh* and *djet* we arrive at the limits of time and also at the question of an eternity beyond all time. For the Egyptians death did not mean a step out of time into eternity. The deceased remained within time; as noted already, they experienced new lifetimes in the underworld and thereby participated in the daily orbit of the sun, a temporal and spatial link between this life and the hereafter. And yet by entering into the afterlife they also enjoyed a divine existence in which different temporal standards or guidelines applied. From this divine perspective, an overview of time extending in many directions was possible; such an overview encompassed the past as well as the future. Thus a hymn from the Ramesside Period praises the god Amun as the creator

> Who oversees the future in millions of years,
> The *djet* is before his eyes
> As yesterday, when it passed.

In Egyptian linguistic usage the future is behind: it is what human beings, oriented toward the past, are as yet unable to see. In contrast, the creator god has an overview of the entire fullness of time. He also can move through time in different directions. On his nocturnal journey through the underworld, for example, he travels backward, from old age to youth, in the form of the time snake. In the work of creation he removed or unhinged the world from atemporality and put it into time. He set a beginning for the *neheh* time, a beginning to which corresponds an end of the world and of time.

The question whether the respective terms for "time" and "eternity" should be treated as synonyms still remains a subject of contro-

The sky goddess Nut in a field of stars, on the
bottom of a Late Period stone sarcophagus.
Musée du Louvre, Paris.

versy. Many researchers contend that the terms should not be used interchangeably, and to support their arguments they attempt to differentiate between the two in a variety of ways: they claim that *djet* is the past and *neheh* the future (A. Gardiner); that *neheh* means this life and *djet* the afterlife (W. Thausing); that *neheh* is eternity prior to creation and *djet* eternity after creation (A. M. Bakir); that *neheh* refers to eternal recurrence of the same and *djet* to invariable constancy (E. Otto); that *neheh* means time and *djet* space (W. Westendorf); or that *neheh* is cyclical time while *djet* is linear (S. Morenz). Suggestive as they may be, some of these definitions are completely groundless, and it is possible to find counterexamples for these and any other distinctions one might propose.

The Egyptians themselves doubtless sensed that the terms had particular sets of associations, as suggested by the following tendencies in usage. *Neheh* is often associated with the day and the sun god, Re; correspondingly, *djet* tends to occur in references to the night and to the ruler of death, Osiris. *Neheh* is often characterized as dynamic, *djet* as static; and as the etymology of the terms reveals, they connote "flow" and "duration" of time, respectively. While such references would seem to support those who argue for clear differentiation between *neheh* and *djet*, there are, however, countless instances in which the two terms are used interchangeably. Thus, even though the Egyptians may well have perceived differences in meaning, such differences are not reflected clearly in their linguistic usage. For this reason, attempts to classify or systematize the differences between *neheh* and *djet* have consistently failed. Here too Egyptian thought resists being fit into a rigid scheme or system. If one still wishes to define the difference between *neheh* and *djet* in contemporary terms, then perhaps it is best to follow Assmann, who distinguishes between "continuity" and "discontinuity" and thereby captures two essential aspects of the Egyptian notion of time.

Neheh and *djet* have spatial connotations as well. The "hidden room" of the afterlife is entirely filled by time, and the deceased wander along paths that extend through space and time alike. According to a well-documented image, *neheh* and *djet* act as supporting pillars for the arc of heaven, and the continued existence of the world depends on them. In the Coffin Texts this function leads to the identification of *neheh* and *djet* with the god Shu, who divided heaven and earth at the time of the creation, and his sister Tefnut. The Book of the Celestial Cow from the Amarna Period depicts them as living pillars supporting the heavens; they appear for the first time here as a divine couple, and thereby help create a compelling visual image of the indivisible unity of time and space that came into being at the time of creation.

Just as heaven and earth determine and embody the spatial structure of the created world, *neheh* and *djet* give it its temporal shape. Together they represent the entire supply of time available to the world; they are identical with the duration of being. According to the Egyptians, this duration is "millions of years." It is as infinite as the endless body of a snake from which one hour after another is mysteriously born.

The natural wish for more time gave way to another wish, namely, for what has repeatedly been the object of human desire: time "without end," or eternity. This wish went hand in hand with the dark certainty that the supply of time is not unlimited, and that at some unforeseeable point it will come to an end. The structure of the world will collapse, and as the unsupported sky crashes to earth again, it will stop the course of the sun god, whose lifetime is defined as *neheh* and *djet*, the entire expanse of being. In keeping with the dualistic thinking of the Egyptians, even this totality is differentiated into two terms: terms that are separate, but that only in conjunction produce the whole. Ancient visitors to Egypt were awestruck by the temporal horizon that opened before them in archives and reports by Egyptian priests. The records of nine thousand years that (according to Plato) they showed to Solon correspond roughly to the 341 generations spoken of by Herodotus (II, 142). The original records of the Turin Canon from the New Kingdom cover approximately forty thousand years since the creation, and include a prehistory with entire dynasties of gods and demigods who precede the historical kings. Juxtaposed to this closed-off, archived past lie the millions of years of the open-ended future.

Compared with such vast time periods, the individual's life on earth seemed nothing more than a passing dream. But while the Egyptians recognized life's brevity, they also knew that in the final analysis what mattered was not the quantity but the quality of a person's lifetime; meaningfully filled time was ultimately of far greater importance than empty duration. On a Dynasty 22 statue of a priest from Karnak, the value of the moment is praised in the following unsurpassable way:

A moment when one sees the rays of the sun
is more valuable than being the eternal lord of the underworld.

These are astonishing words for a culture that created works for eternity. According to medieval Arabic author al-Jamani "even time was frightened" by the buildings of the Egyptians. In their calm, self-assured stance in the face of all transitoriness, the Egyptians seem to have overcome time itself.

Each beginning, whether a seasonal change, a new ruler's ascent to power, or a *sed* festival, offered the chance to use time in a new and better way—to "fill" it, as the Egyptians say. Wise teachers caution that to "fill" means to "fill properly." Time should be neither just barely full nor filled to the point of overflowing. Ptahhotep, author of the best-known of the ancient Egyptian "instructions," instructs his pupil to use only what is necessary for daily household tasks and to "follow his heart" the rest of the time.

The same attitude echoes in harpists' songs, which since the Amarna Period urged listeners to enjoy the pleasures of this life. Significantly, they recommend seeking pleasure not despite its transitoriness but precisely because of it. "Celebrate a holiday," runs the refrain. The moment is elevated and time becomes a vessel for a filled and fulfilling present. The impact of what was accomplished along the Nile of antiquity derives at least in part from this conscious and conscientious fashioning of time.

CHAPTER 4

L I M I T S

A N D

S Y M M E T R I E S

LIKE their concept of time, the ancient Egyptians' notion of spatial limits or borders entails two distinct words. Unlike *neheh* and *djet*, however, these terms can be clearly defined. *Tash* refers to borders set by humans or gods within the confines of the world. These borders can be extended and crossed. *Djer* refers to the absolute, unalterable limit that is part of the cosmic structure itself. By analogy, we might describe *tash* as the speed limit in a given geographical area, and *djer* as the speed of light.

The Egyptians used *tash* for structuring devices and measures of all kinds. The term might refer to the boundary of a field or piece of property, or to district or state borders; in the Late Period, during the first century B.C., it also meant an area defined by such borders. The term occurs in connection with numbers and counting, and appears in writing as the classifying sign of two crossed staffs. *Djer*, on the other hand, is indicated with the sign for "path."

‹ Quartzite statue of an unnamed official, from
Gebelaw, Upper Egypt, Dynasty 6. The Metropolitan
Museum of Art, New York.

Each pharaoh upon coming to power found predetermined limits everywhere—national borders, the borders of districts and other administrative units, the borders of cities, the borders of temple precincts. As far as the larger, national borders, we need to ask two questions: How are they defined, and how firmly are they defined? Egypt has clearly recognizable geographical boundaries on all sides: the Mediterranean to the north, the mountainous desert of the Sinai Peninsula and the Red Sea to the east, the vast expanse of the Libyan Desert to the west, and in the south the granite barrier of the first Nile cataract at Aswan, an almost insurmountable obstacle to further navigation of the river. Each of these represents an obvious natural boundary, but such boundaries are not absolute. A people bounded by an ocean may cross the water to distant shores, as the Greeks and Vikings demonstrated; and as we see from Arab and Mongol cultures, a desert people can extend its grasp to fruitful areas beyond the barrenness of its immediate surroundings.

From the Old Kingdom on, the Egyptians reached beyond their country's natural boundaries with expeditions that were organized carefully and carried out with great effort. They traversed the neighboring desert areas of Libya, Nubia, and the Sinai, and sailed across the sea to Lebanon and distant African coasts (Punt, perhaps modern Somaliland) to open and develop new avenues for trade. Such expeditions led to the establishment of new political boundaries, but only at a much later date. The Egyptians did not erect permanent military bases in Nubia before the Middle Kingdom, for example, and did not govern in Syria, Lebanon, and Palestine until the New Kingdom.

The kings established and marked their extended national boundaries ceremoniously. Border stelae erected in Nubia by the Middle Kingdom pharaoh Senwosret III bear inscriptions intended to reinforce the message of the stelae themselves as border markers. The inscriptions forbade any Nubian to cross the border "by ship or by land" for any purpose other than trade. The text addressed the king's successors in equally solemn tones. They too had obligations concerning the border, since "he who lets himself be driven back from his border is a true coward." Thus the king declared: "Each of my sons who maintains the border that My Majesty has set is my son and is born of My Majesty. The exemplary son protects his father and maintains the boundary of his begetter. He who lets it decline and will not defend it is not my son and is not born of me." By his own order, a statue of the king was erected at the Nubian border just as at other Egyptian national borders. These statues symbolized the pharaoh's constant, watchful presence even at the farthest corners of his lands and dissuaded potential enemies from overstepping the boundary. In the New Kingdom, Tuthmosis I and Tuthmosis III erected stelae on the banks of the Euphrates for the same purpose.

The texts inscribed on border and triumphal stelae threatened punishment, even death, for those who did not respect the boundary. Before a military campaign it was common for the pharaoh to announce that enemies had violated Egypt's borders. By emphasizing the "provocation" and the need for a response, the pharaoh skillfully avoided giving the impression that he was beginning a war of aggression. His borders were sacrosanct. Any attempt to change them would meet with the same ceremonious defense efforts as those used to protect Egyptian religious institutions.

When Akhenaton created his new residence Akhetaten (modern Tell el-Amarna), in the fifth and sixth years of his reign, he erected a total of fourteen border stelae along both banks of the Nile to indicate the extent of his municipal district. He made the following "oath of truth": "The southern stela that stands on the eastern mountain of Akhetaten is a stela of Akhetaten that I shall leave in place. For all eternity I shall not go beyond it to the south." Comparable formulations are found on the western, eastern, and northern stelae. Earlier scholars interpreted this oath as a commitment on Akhenaton's part to remain permanently within the boundaries of his new capital. His text, however, continues with precise measurements and allocation of the area to Aton. Along both sides of the Nile, the farthest stelae delimited a stretch of land of more than six Egyptian miles. The area between the stelae—which included "mountains, deserts, and fields; with new land, highland, and fresh land; with water and inhabited areas, shore, people, and animals; with trees and all other things"—was declared the property of Akhenaton and his "father" Aton. In other words, the new residential area was a religious site dedicated to a god, with borders firmly established once and for all, never to be altered.

The geographical area overseen and partially controlled by the Egyptians was organized symmetrically. It contained a "divine land" in the north (Lebanon) and a corresponding one in the south (Punt); there were both an Upper Egyptian and a Lower Egyptian Heliopolis, and Behedet and Busiris also occurred twice. To the sky above corresponded a "counterheaven" below the earth's surface, and the landscape of the Egyptian underworld provided a mirror image of that on earth, complete with canals, fertile pastures, desert regions, and River Nile. Even the skilled workers in the Deir el-Medina settlement employed in the royal tombs and other official building projects were divided into two symmetrical "halves," each group with its own foreman, and the structure of the entire administration reflected the division of Upper and Lower Egypt.

The symmetry implied by two corresponding halves characterized Egyptian art as well. The majority of temples in Egypt and Nubia were axial in plan: one central axis served as the reference for symmetrically arranged rows of rooms and building parts whose num-

bers could be increased at will. Stelae, false doors, statues, and sarcophagus decoration all gave a similar impression of perfect
symmetry that nonetheless rarely appears severe or lifeless.

The liveliness we sense within a rigidly organized overall scheme
has a simple explanation. What initially appears to be complete symmetry reveals itself upon closer examination as a sophisticated, carefully thought-out arrangement that incorporates minor deviations
from the given pattern. At least one student of Egyptian art in the
nineteenth century realized that such deviations were intentional. Sir
Gardner Wilkinson spoke disparagingly of the Egyptians' "symme-
trophobia," but the Prussian traveler Hermann Prince Pückler-
Muskau recognized that the slight deviations or variations were precisely what made the use of symmetry here so masterly.

Pückler-Muskau's insight found little resonance. In the scholarly
literature such deviations were generally called errors, and were attributed to the artist's or scribe's carelessness. In 1940, Alfred Hermann revised this judgment, when he interpreted the slight artistic
deviations as a deliberate means of avoiding complete sterility and
mechanical repetition. As his starting point Hermann chose the or-
namental inscription of Crocodilopolis in the Faiyum, which had
been made in Dynasty 12 for King Amenemhat III. The two halves
of the inscription that flank a central column of signs correspond to
each other in every detail but one: on the right side, the sign group for
"beloved" faces the "wrong" direction.

Scholars have identified many comparable examples of deliberate
deviation from a symmetrical arrangement in Egyptian art. Not all in-
volve the reversal of a sign group in an arrangement of symmetrically
written characters. Sometimes the addition or subtraction of an individual sign disturbs the symmetry, and helps create a less rigid sense
of visual balance. In larger works, deviation occurs in accompanying

Stela of Ahmose, first king of Dynasty 18, from
Abydos. Cairo Museum. The stela commemo-
rates the construction of a funerary monument
for Ahmose's grandmother Tetishery. The symmetrical duplicated image above shows the king
before his grandmother, and below is tran-
scribed a rather unusual conversation between
Ahmose and his queen-sister, Ahmose Nofretari. The king says that although Tetishery already has a tomb and a cenotaph, he wishes to
erect a pyramid and vault in her memory in the
necropolis at Abydos. "Never," says the text,
"had the kings of former times done such a thing
for their mothers."

texts or images whose regular alternating pattern is interrupted at some point. Even amid the richly decorated capitals of the columns in the pronaos of the Ptolemaic Period temple at Edfu, a single deviation breaks an otherwise strictly maintained symmetrical order.

In such cases we obviously cannot speak of chance or error. In 1986, Sylvia Schoske argued that Egyptian sculpture likewise shows conscious deviation from absolute symmetry. In high-quality Egyptian sculpture the respective axes of nose and eyebrows do not form a precise right angle, the mouth may be slightly off center, or the two sides of a head covering may not be the same width. The more asymmetrical a portrait head is, the stronger the sense of individual personality it conveys. Only in periods of artistic decline and stagnation did the Egyptians seem to prefer a more rigid, mechanical type of symmetry.

The avoidance of complete symmetry reflects a more comprehensive underlying principle found in many different aspects of Egyptian culture, including the writing system. Although they employed certain written conventions, the Egyptians had no single binding orthography and never decided definitively in favor of a purely alphabetical writing system. Through graphic dissimilation and color variation, and by continual variation in the writing of individual signs, they

Symmetrical inscription of Amenemhat III, Dynasty 12.

Wood, stone, and metal statue of Imertnates,
priestess of Amun, Dynasty 12. Rijksmuseum
van Oudheden, Leiden.

Statue of the wife of Maya, Tutankhamun's treasurer.
Rijksmuseum van Oudheden, Leiden.

avoided monotony in the same way that a visual artist might create variety even in a long series of images or with repeated motifs. The possibilities for combining recurring visual motifs seem virtually unlimited. Equally impressive for their imaginative variations on basic patterns are Egyptian hymns to the sun and their metrically arranged texts.

By evading rigid schemes and fixed rules, the Egyptians went against precisely those ordering principles that modern science strives to uphold. Overly schematic modern attempts at interpretation prove incompatible with ancient Egyptian sources and fail to promote genuine understanding. While they eschewed complete symmetry, the Egyptians also avoided the opposite extreme of sheer randomness and the dissolution of all order. Their ideal was to follow a middle course of lively yet careful deviation from a set pattern—and that ideal was closely related to their notion of ongoing regeneration.

They worked toward achieving and maintaining a delicate balance between the preservation and variation of the given; in the Egyptian view, striking such a balance was essential for reasonable progress to be made. This concept of balance generated another fundamental principle of Egyptian thought and practice, and reintroduced the concept of boundaries. While the Egyptians carefully established boundaries and threatened to punish anyone who violated them, in certain cases they deliberately overstepped those limits. In the New Kingdom, the same pharaoh who warned others not to cross his borders often bore the epithet "he who extends Egypt's boundaries." He thus not only preserved his inheritance but also enlarged it, as we learn from inscriptions with vivid, detailed accounts of how each king, at least in principle, surpassed all his predecessors' achievements.

I call this impulse, which has a tangible influence on the pharaoh's actions, a principle of "extension of the existing." Although most eas-

Dynasty 18 statue of Senenmut, who enfolds his
official charge Nefrure, sole heir of Hatshepsut.
British Museum, London.

ily identified in source materials from the New Kingdom, the principle was doubtless in effect in the Old Kingdom. We see it with particular clarity when we consider historical developments in the layout
of royal and nonroyal tombs: what may look like a regressive tendency (similar to the gradual reduction in pyramid size from Dynasty
4 onward) is actually a shift of emphasis. Extension or expansion does
take place, but it occurs in new areas such as the decoration of places
of worship.

Beginning in the First Intermediate Period, Egyptian rulers expressed quite openly their desire to "extend the existing." In Dynasty
10, for example, the father of the regional King Merikare wished for
a successor who would outstrip him and "increase what I have
achieved." Senwosret in Dynasty 12 could assert: "I have increased
what was passed down to me"; and Tuthmosis I in Dynasty 18: "I do
more than other kings before me have done." The young Tutankhamun "went beyond what had been done since the time of his ancestors."

While such formulations are obviously set phrases, even in the case
of Tutankhamun, who died at an early age, they retain some corre-
spondence to reality. The inscription on Tutankhamun's "restoration
stela" instructed that the number of poles used to carry a processional
image of Amun be increased from eleven to thirteen. Tutankhamun
ordered also that the number of carrying poles for the image of Ptah
be increased from seven to eleven, as Ptah's importance now approached that of Amun. Such subtleties may seem trivial to us today,
but like the number of sacrificial offerings and feast days to honor the
gods, the number of carrying poles played a significant role in the cul-
tic and markedly religious political life of the pharaonic kingdom.
Here we see a concrete, specific application of the ideological require-
ment to "extend the existing."

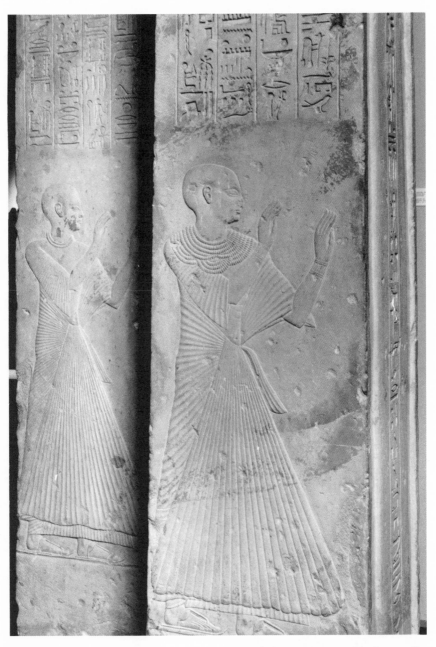

Jambs from the doorway of the Dynasty 19
tomb of Ptahmose at Saqqara. Rijksmuseum
van Oudheden, Leiden.

In temple construction this principle took on decidedly more grandiose proportions. As noted above, the basic floor plan of the axial temple not only allowed for continual additions, but even encouraged them; in fact, Egyptian temples were never fully completed. Each pharaoh was intent on adding to his predecessors' work. Often the additions were restricted to a modest, even symbolic expansion, but the heavy concentration on building projects in the early years of each king's reign testifies to the strength of this impulse to expand. The same impulse informs the ritual military campaigns that marked the beginning of a new government; we will return to these rituals in connection with the topic of history as celebration.

The royal rock tombs of the New Kingdom represent one of the clearest applications of the rule of expansion. The oldest tombs in the Valley of the Kings, dating from the reign of Tuthmosis I, around 1490 B.C., had few rooms and modest proportions. As one government gave way to another, however, not only did the tombs increase in overall size, but also they acquired more rooms, more supporting pillars, and more elaborate decoration. The expansion culminated in the burial palaces of the Ramesside Period, which extended more than one hundred meters down into the limestone rock and were decorated throughout with colorful reliefs.

A careful analysis of the floor plan, decoration, and measurements shows that as each new period of government began, the king's tomb was reorganized, redecorated, and systematically enlarged. A canon of royal dimensions was used exclusively for the king's tomb, and a number of decorative motifs were likewise reserved for it; not even in the tomb of a queen do we find these particular elements. A pillar in the king's tomb measured exactly two cubits square, and beginning with Amenophis III the floor space in a corridor measured five cubits square (1 royal cubit equals 52.3 centimeters). If other tombs included pillars, they had to differ noticeably in size from those in the king's tomb.

In the tomb of Queen Tausert (circa 1190 B.C.), it is possible to trace the changes in her official status over the course of her life. She began as a normal queen under Sety II, was ruler of the land under the young Siptah, and finally became the ruling pharaoh. Correspondingly, her tomb was initially constructed as that of a queen, but was later enlarged to include a sarcophagus chamber with pillars and royal decoration, although it still did not have the measurements reserved for a king's tomb. These too finally appeared, but only in a second, unfinished sarcophagus chamber.

For more than three hundred years in the New Kingdom the pharaohs attempted to join new elements with more traditional basic concepts in their burial chambers. In the process, the canon of royal measurements continually changed. Sarcophagus chambers became larger, corridors longer and higher. The rooms became more numerous, the decoration more abundant. With Ramesses III (1184–1153 B.C.), the expansion reached its apparent limit. By this time the king's tomb had become so elaborate that further additions may have seemed impossible, or perhaps simply impractical. Around 1150 B.C., Ramesses IV shortened his tomb radically, limited it to several rooms, and eliminated pillars and many basic decorative elements as well. Yet even he could not resist the impulse to "extend the existing" altogether: he built corridors noticeably higher and wider than in earlier tombs.

By studying the tombs in the Valley of the Kings we see how a boundary that at first was set only tentatively, and that later underwent many alterations and extensions, ultimately evolved into a limit that the Egyptians considered final. In the face of such limits Egyptian planners devised many sophisticated ways to exploit what little room remained, but eventually every human effort confronted absolute, inexorable boundaries belonging to the structure of the world itself. These boundaries were known as *djer*, or end. The Egyptians reconfirmed a limit even as they extended it; an analogous concept exists in the ethical realm, where the principle of *maat* determined all attainable limits.

The desire to supersede all that has come before and to perform incomparable feats acquired a heretofore unknown intensity with the establishment of an Egyptian empire in Dynasty 18. Architecture and sculpture tended toward monumentality. There were athletic achievements on the part of the pharaoh, which in Wolfgang Decker's view closely resemble modern record-setting: the athletic events took place before witnesses; they were carefully measured, and then recorded for posterity.

Dynasty 18 kings liked to name concrete, geographically precise boundaries for their kingdom in official inscriptions. Amenophis III ruled an area "whose southern border extends to Karoy [by the fourth Nile cataract], and whose northern border reaches as far as Naharina [Syria]." His predecessor Tuthmosis I could proudly declare his northern border to be the Euphrates (known in Egypt as "the reversed water" because it flows in the opposite direction from the Nile).

Such precise descriptions, however, were far less popular than figurative, even mythical descriptions of the extent of the pharaoh's rule. Among these boundaries were the "earth's horn" to the south, and the "Asian swamp holes" to the north; the mountainous region of Nubia and the lagoons of the northern Nile delta form natural borders for Egypt that in certain formulaic expressions became idealized borders of the world. In topographical terms, such borders are somewhat vague. The "swamp holes," for instance, became increasingly remote as the Egyptian world view expanded. They receded from the delta farther north and eventually were "located" in Asia Minor, which in fact was anything but marshland. Other New Kingdom expressions described the king's rule as extending "to the wind" in the south, that is, as far as the north wind blew, and "to the ends of the ocean" in the north, or "as far as the primeval darkness," or "to the supports of heaven." With these and other expressions the Egyptians attempted to define their entire world, right up to the very limits of existence. One of the simplest characterizations for this vast expanse is the expression "that which the sun orbits"; another is in the words of praise used by the viceroy Seny for the god Khnum: "to the heights of the heavens, the breadth of the earth, the depth of the sea." It is significant that only the deceased could utilize these distances fully. In comparison with this life, life after death acquired new, expanded dimensions; in the Egyptian view it spanned the entire cosmos.

Even so, the absolute farthest limits remain unknown to gods and deceased alike. This we learn from the Book of Nut, a description of heaven dating from the thirteenth century B.C. The Book of Nut speaks of distant regions never touched by the sun, of areas that remain in eternal darkness and thereby belong to the world before creation. The ultimate limit can be only limitlessness. "Darkness," "primeval ocean," and "profound depths" are merely descriptions of what is actually formless, unstructured, and unlimited, of that from which the world emerged. Temporally as well as spatially, the created world borders everywhere on the uncreated and nonexisting; this fact is expressed perhaps most clearly in the image of the ouroboros, the snake that bites its own tail and returns into itself.

By its very nature this type of border is diffuse and ultimately incomprehensible. Re travels toward it on the primeval water of Nun, yet that same water limits the sun god's progress on all sides. It encircles the world and extends outward in all directions into infinity. The

Dynasty 13 sculpture which originally showed a
man, his son, and grandson, all priests of Ptah at
Memphis. Musée du Louvre, Paris.

darkness is no different: although the sun's path through the under-world is illuminated every night, and differentiated from the dark-ness, the underworld as a whole remains essentially dark. Spell 175 in the Book of the Dead calls it "completely deep, completely dark, com-pletely eternal," and in the Book of Caves its ruler, Osiris, is a god "whose head . . . and whose back side [are] in darkness."

While they existed already before creation, primeval darkness and water together represent a border or limit that is also tangible. The dark floodwaters of the Nile come from this source, as does the noc-turnal darkness, and sleepers descend into depths where they encoun-ter both gods and the deceased. The created world is by no means clearly separated from the uncreated. The border becomes fluid time and again, the process of creation continues, and boundlessness has at once a salutary and threatening effect.

In ancient Egypt we find the yearning for limitation side by side with the desire to transcend and dissolve all boundaries. Both are pro-foundly human desires, and the Egyptians' ability to fulfill both con-tributed greatly to the sense of balance that characterizes their culture as a whole. The Egyptian world was carefully ordered in every re-spect, with clearly set limits that everyone was expected to honor. Meaningful, sensible limits grow out of experience; they provide helpful guidance rather than arbitrary, restrictive measures.

The Egyptians never abandoned the belief that it was possible to change the world in productive ways; in their view, it was always pos-sible to bring a negative or imperfect condition back—or at least closer—to its perfect state at the time of creation. Ancient Egyptian culture derived a remarkable energy and optimism from this belief; their perspective on life had no room for fatalism or for a passive, un-questioning acceptance of the status quo.

This attitude did not even accept death as a limit. Rather than signal the end of life, death marked a transition to a new existence with greater potential. The dead were considered "alive"; their ruler, Osiris, was called "king of the living," and the expression "life after death" occurred often in Egyptian wishes. When the deceased entered the world of the gods, they blended with them and became gods themselves. The narrow limits set for them on earth disappeared. Living and acting as gods in the broad expanse of the sky and in the depths of the earth, their only boundaries were those of existence itself. Egyptian texts about the afterlife describe how the deceased person, as a member of the sun god's entourage, ventures to the farthest points of the sun's orbit and thereby arrives at the beginning of nonbeing.

CHAPTER 5

THE

HEREAFTER

A JOURNEY to the dead follows the course of
the sun, beginning with the evening sunset. Fading from sight and
leaving this world behind, the sun carries its light down into invisible
depths; after traversing the Realm of the Dead it emerges revitalized
each morning. These daily occurrences are the basis of the Egyptians'
firm belief that during the night the deceased enjoy the light of the
sun, and that death represents merely a transition to a new, rejuvenated form of life.

The nocturnal sun shines on the dead, awakening them to new life.
Its light makes it possible to see in the otherwise inaccessible dark
chambers below the earth's surface, and at least begin to fathom the
underlying structure of the space where the visions of the unconscious
meet the world of dreams. The Egyptians were the first to practice a
Jungian psychology of archetypes and to recognize the fundamental
restorative power of the unconscious. They realized that in sleep and
dreams, one experiences these depths as a psychic reality in which one
may encounter gods and the deceased alike.

Sleepers and dreamers enter the primeval ocean of Nun that serves as a waterway for the barge of the sun, as it sinks on the western horizon each evening. These watery depths have three different aspects: they are at once the watery sphere of the primeval ocean, the earthly depths of the underworld, and the heavenly realm above. The celestial goddess Nut swallows the sun in the evening and allows it to wander through her body until it is born anew in the morning; at the same time, the sun traverses the Netherworld, realm of the earth gods Aker, Geb, and Tatenen, and simultaneously proceeds through the floods of Nun on a journey through the body of a crocodile, which the Egyptians considered the most powerful aquatic animal. Within Egyptian thought and imagery, there is no contradiction in this threefold conception. The different descriptions serve as complementary representations of the same journey through the threatening yet regenerating depths of the world.

Our sources of information about the sun's descent and ascent date back to Old Kingdom Pyramid Texts and include writings from as late as the Greco-Roman Period. In a collection of New Kingdom religious texts, the Egyptians seem increasingly systematic in their exploration of the sun's voyage. Known as the Books of the Netherworld, these texts used to be characterized as "guides to the Beyond." They include the Amduat, the Book of Gates, the Book of Caverns, and the Book of Earth. Their ancient generic designation "books about what is in *dat*" indicates their aim: to provide information usually from the standpoint of the sun god and his companions about the underworld, *dat*, its inhabitants, and its topography in both written and pictorial form. The numerous illustrations for these texts in the tombs in Valley of the Kings testify to the New Kingdom flowering of Egyptian book painting.

The Books of the Netherworld were initially intended solely for the tomb of a king. Only around 1000 B.C., in the Theban "divine state of Amun" (Dynasty 21), did higher priests of Amun appropriate this royal privilege for their own sarcophagi and burial papyri. Notations emphasize that the texts are esoteric writings: only the pharaoh, as the son of the sun god and the earthly sun, knows all the secrets connected with the sun's course and the underworld. Whereas the spells in the Book of the Dead give practical advice for the afterlife, the Books of the Netherworld are meant to help expand the Egyptians' knowledge about the nocturnal side of life.

These books attempt to follow the sun from the time it sets to the time it rises once again, and thereby trace a path that leads backward through time and space. As the sun moves from west to east along its nightly route, it is transformed from an old man into a child. The essence of the underworld comes into view as the sun's light makes objects in the underworld visible and the light of consciousness allows the contents of the unconscious to surface. The texts also refer clearly to areas beyond the course of the sun; never penetrated—or even touched—by the light of consciousness, such regions rest in eternal darkness.

The older Books of the Netherworld (the Amduat and the Book of Gates) describe the Beyond as divided spatially into twelve units corresponding to the twelve hours required for the sun's journey. Massive gates protected by serpents and terrifying demons separate the individual hourly segments, each of which consists of three registers. The passing sun god in his barge appears in the middle register. In the later texts (the Book of Caves and the Book of the Earth) this organization becomes less rigid. The vessel of the sun gives way to the solar disk, which in most scenes implies the presence of the celestial body.

Below the horizon, the depths are divided into three parts. The thin, uppermost level crossed by the sun in the first nocturnal hour is a middle ground between this life and the hereafter. Before reaching the first gate to the underworld, one must go past a row of jubilant baboons and other creatures in this space. The Amduat gives precise measurements in Egyptian miles for this level, which corresponds to the first three nocturnal hours, as if to suggest that one can fathom at least this portion of the depths before having to abandon measurements altogether. A corresponding buffer zone precedes the sunrise.

After this first region of transition comes the actual underworld, or *dat*. Flowing through the center of the Netherworld is a river whose water belongs to the primordial water of Nun. It serves as the waterway for the sun, and as a main thoroughfare for traffic it represents the underworld counterpart of the Nile. Along the riverbanks, gods and the blessed dead cry out joyfully and extend their hands to touch the tow rope of the barge. Encircled by a protective serpent, the sun god on his barge appears as a human figure with a ram's head. Although

The sun god Re accompanied by divinities on his barge, from the Amduat in the tomb of Tuthmosis III, Valley of the Kings.

Amun, Khnum, and other gods are depicted similarly in afterlife scenes, the ram-headed figure refers hieroglyphically to the god's descent into the depths as a *ba*, or soul, that will unite with its body in the underworld.

In the Amduat the sun god is accompanied by an entire throng of divinities, among them Wepwawet, who acts as "opener of the ways"; Hathor, "mistress" of the barge; and Horus, its helmsman. In the Book of Gates, only the two creative powers Sia and Heka (perception and magic, respectively) are along to aid the sun god as he exercises his creative powers in the nocturnal underworld. Not only did he establish the world in the beginning, but he also renews it daily.

The sun god's power extends only to a certain point. Far below the region that he fills with light and his creative word lies the third and lowest level of the underworld, the "place of destruction" (*hetemit*). It is an invisible, completely dark, bottomless abyss beyond all creation, a place "not to be entered." Spell 175 in the Book of the Dead refers to the underworld as "completely deep, completely dark, completely unending." Its farthest depths are filled by the same primordial darkness that preceded creation.

This region bears the name "place of destruction" for an obvious reason. It is inhabited by forces that destroy and dissolve everything entering their domain. In the Books of the Netherworld the business of destruction is carried out in countless scenes depicting the punishment of enemies—an activity shown most often in the lower registers, since these lie closest to the actual underworld depths. Here the destructive imagination knows no bounds.

Hostile creatures whose evil deeds have led to their conviction at the Judgment of the Dead are bound, decapitated, and set on fire; their hearts are torn from their bodies, their heads placed at their own feet. The destruction of the body also marks the destruction of the *ba*;

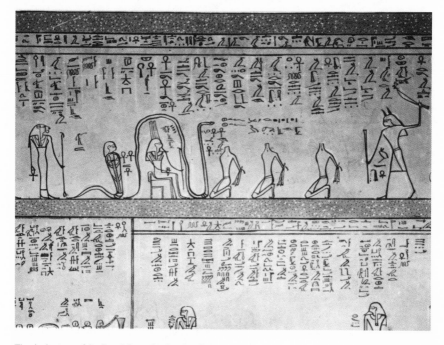

The Judgment of the Dead, from the Amduat in
the tomb of Amenophis II, Valley of the Kings.
Osiris, enthroned and ringed by the *mehen*
snake, oversees the punishment of enemies by a
god with cat ears.

it effaces the shadows of the condemned, and relegates their names to
oblivion, to nonexistence. One scene in the Book of Gates shows a tremendous serpent, "the fiery one," breathing on bound sinners before
it and setting them on fire; we meet similar fire-breathing snakes with
practically every step in the Egyptian underworld. Other scenes depict
fire-filled pits or the ominous Lake of Fire. The condemned experience the lake's red water as a burning liquid that brings the total destruction of both body and soul.

In the Book of Caves, knife-wielding demons heat caldrons that
contain the condemned, or sometimes dissolved parts of their person-

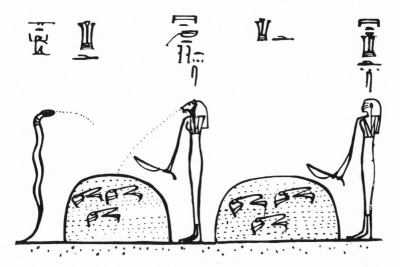

The snake "who burns millions," and deities spitting fire into the graves of the condemned, from the Amduat in the tomb of Tuthmosis III, Valley of the Kings.

alities. By boiling the condemned persons until they are tender, the demons prepare them for the state of nonbeing. An image dating from the Roman Period combines this punishment with the Judgment of the Dead. The caldron motif, like many other Egyptian conceptions about infernal punishments, lives on in the Christian Middle Ages.

The Judgment of the Dead is itself an ancient Egyptian concept, although it does not occur as a visual image until Dynasty 18. The image associated with the trial is that of the scale that weighs an individual's heart against *maat*, or order. In the Amarna Period, the Devourer of the Dead is depicted crouching menacingly beside the scale as the visible maw of hell, ready to consume the condemned. In a single figure that combines features of lion, hippopotamus, and crocodile, this creature embodies the nameless dangers that threaten all who descend into the depths of the underworld. The Litany of Re speaks of terrible creatures "who sever heads and slit throats, who clutch at hearts and tear them from breasts, who stage a bloodbath."

At the punishment sites, where no sun shines and no breath of life stirs, where hearing and sight fade away and being itself is shattered, one comes face to face with the threat of final extinction. One stands before the black hole of nonbeing, in which the world will dissolve at the end of time. This is represented in a hieroglyph as a circle filled in with black. Yet, the Egyptians recognized, dissolution and extinction are the prerequisites for each new creation; renewed life must be preceded by a period of decay. Rotting and decay therefore take on a distinctly positive character. The world of the afterlife presents two faces. It is an empire of unending promise in which even the impossible becomes possible, and a source of continual regeneration for all that ex-

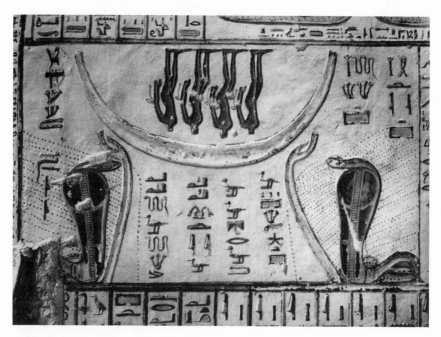

Upside-down decapitated bodies in a caldron
heated by fire-spitting snakes, from the Book of
Caverns in the tomb of Ramesses VI, Valley of the Kings.

ists. At the same time it represents a horror-filled abyss, compellingly described in spell 99B of the Book of the Dead as "this terrible land where overturned stars fall on their faces, and know not how to raise themselves again."

In the figure of Osiris, who was murdered and dismembered by his brother Seth, mortality receives its most brutal expression. But Osiris comes back to life to become not only the ruler of the underworld but also a model for all the deceased. In addition, Osiris's sister-wife, Isis, conceives Horus from his dead body. As Horus emerges from that decayed body, he attests to the continuity of life: the germ of life can be passed on even beyond the threshold of death. Osiris's fate incorporates both the weakness and the triumph of the physical. The material body disintegrates into dust, but the annual rebirth seen in nature each spring bears witness to the body's ultimate triumph over death.

The belief that the body lives on after death is one of the most salient features of Egyptian conceptions of the hereafter. The lively scenes of eating and drinking, music and dance, the pleasures of love and free, unimpaired movement found in Egyptian tombs reflect a concerted effort to guarantee the continuation of this existence. The Egyptians hoped that beyond death they would enjoy an active, productive life, one that would even include work, in the verdant fields of the hereafter. They wished to be free only of the drudgery of watering and working the fields, and for this reason included among their burial objects statuettes known as shawabties. When magically activated, these figurines would relieve them of burdensome chores, and allow them to sow, plow, and harvest without effort.

By the beginning of the Old Kingdom, and for more than three thousand years, the Egyptians carefully prepared the bodies of the dead for burial as mummies. But the deceased were rarely depicted in this mummified state, as the Egyptians did not wish to live on in a re-

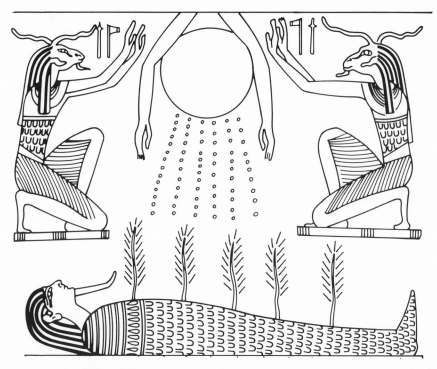

The sun's rays awaken the mummy of Osiris to
new life. Drawing from a Dynasty 21 coffin in the
Fitzwilliam Museum, Cambridge, England.

stricted, immobile condition. Rather, they hoped for a transfigured
body that resembled its earthly counterpart yet surpassed it in both
size and abilities. Although once again fully functional, this afterlife
body would be free of all earthly shortcomings; it would even repeatedly "rejuvenate itself in the tomb." All the physical infirmities nor-
mally associated with old age would be overcome in the renewed
body. Missing limbs would regenerate themselves, a severed head
even rejoin its torso. The unlimited capacity for change and regeneration is the foundation for all ancient Egyptian beliefs about the here-

after. These beliefs are more important than pyramids or funerary temples. Even the majority of the population, who could not afford the extravagance of a decorated tomb or a carefully prepared mummy and sarcophagus with many burial objects, could live with this hope.

In the tenth hour of the Amduat, and also in the ninth hour of the Book of Gates, a large blue rectangle represents the primeval, ubiquitous water of Nun that fills the underworld. Here drift the naked, helpless bodies of individuals who have been deprived of a proper burial; they are neither mummified nor accompanied by burial objects. And yet by passing through the Nile, and with it the water of Nun, they gain direct access to the underworld and thereby escape final destruction and decay. In the Late Period the Egyptians formally recognized the process of "divinization by drowning"; monuments were even erected for people who had drowned in the Nile. The Egyptians could thus rest assured that an elaborate, official burial was not the crucial prerequisite for a blessed afterlife. It was, however, generally considered a wise precaution to build a tomb, a "house for eternity," in good time and to entrust one's body to embalmers who would transform it into a secure shell for the long and treacherous journey to a new home in the afterlife.

The desired regeneration in the Beyond rests on a physical impossibility: the reversal of time. This reversal can be experienced only psychologically as renewal in the depths of the unconscious, or by drifting in the primeval substance of Nun. Here it is possible to bring the irrevocable aging process of the world to a halt; it is even possible—if only temporarily—to reverse its course. The final nocturnal hour of the Amduat gives perhaps the most impressive verbal and pictorial descriptions of this remarkable process in a scene in which the sun god, together with all gods and blessed dead, is pulled backward through the body of an enormous serpent, the symbol of time. Of spe-

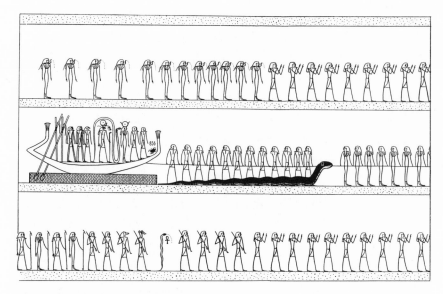

The twelfth and final hour of the Amduat, when the sun god rejuvenates himself by entering the body of a traveling snake. Tomb of Ramesses VI, Valley of the Kings.

cial importance is the change in appearance the voyagers undergo. They enter the serpent's tail as venerable, gray-haired, infirm individuals whose lives are essentially over, and they emerge from the serpent's mouth as young children. The Book of Gates puts this scene in the third nocturnal hour, where the sun's barge is pulled through an elongated serpentine form that signifies the entire underworld with its two entrances, depicted as steer heads. The same basic principle also informs later Books of the Netherworld, which contain strictly symbolic representations of the sun's barge on the back of Aker, the two-headed earth god who stands for the underworld.

In the Amduat, the arms of the god Shu raise the sun into the sky at the end of its journey so that it can reappear in this world and begin its diurnal course once more. The Book of Gates develops the event into a complex scene showing the sun's barge on the arms of Nun, emerging from the primeval waters. The celestial goddess Nut extends her arms toward the craft from above, and Osiris, who encircles the underworld and welcomes the sun each evening back into his realm, also appears. In the Book of Gates the entire course of the sun's daily travels is condensed into this single image.

After the Amarna Period such images occur in the Book of the Dead. The invisible forces that propel the sun and keep it from tumbling into the depths also help the deceased endure the trials of the underworld. Comprehensive depictions of the motif show the sun in continuous motion between two pair of arms representing forces or powers. Almost without exception the force that originates in the depths is male, while the upper force often has the female attribute of a pair of breasts. Besides suggesting the goddess Nut, this attribute refers to the goddess of the West and to Hathor, whose arms extend toward the sun god from the western mountains. In contrast, the power of the depths—regardless of whether it appears as darkness, primordial water, earth, or Osiris—has no maternal, protective character; rather, it is a creative, transforming power.

Like the sun, human beings belong to both upper and lower realms. While their birdlike souls (*ba*s) are pulled toward the sky, their bodies and shadows remain earthbound. Of crucial importance to the Egyptians is that no part, physical or spiritual, of a human being ever completely disappears. What death temporarily separates must be reunited in the afterlife, since only a whole, intact human being can experience reawakening. This unity brings forth new life; it too derives from the course of the sun. The sun god himself descends into the Netherworld as a *ba*, and in so doing carries with him the *ba*s of all other gods and the blessed dead so that they can imbue their material shells with a new spirit.

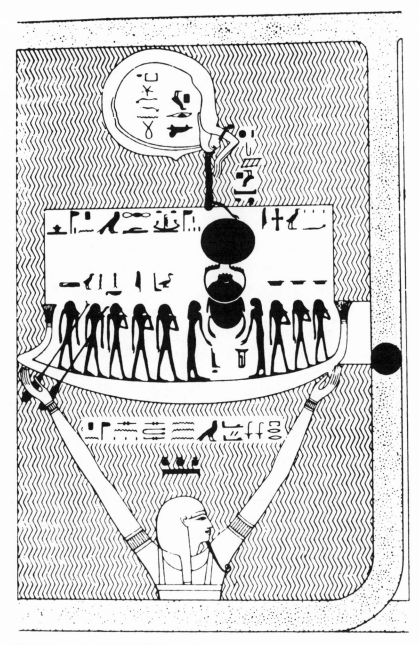

The final scene from the Book of Gates, on the
alabaster sarcophagus of Sety I. Sir John Soane
Museum, London.

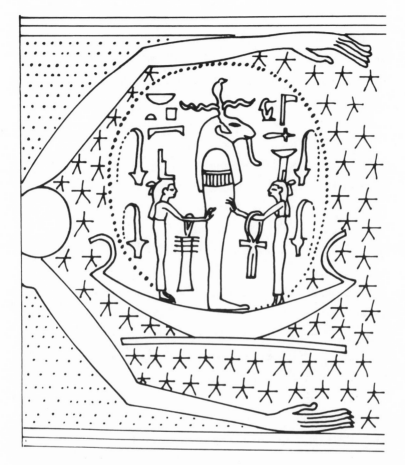

The united image of Re and Osiris, from the
Dynasty 21 Papyrus of Tentamun.

The idea that the sun god Re becomes a *ba* offered New Kingdom
theologians a new solution to a long-standing problem: how to explain adequately the relation between Re, who as the nocturnal sun
spends time in the underworld, and Osiris, the ruler of this same underworld. According to the newfound explanation, Re himself becomes the *ba* of Osiris. Uniting with the body of the underworld god

each night, he penetrates him completely with his light and thereby awakens new life. Written texts, as well as visual images, from the tomb of Nofretari on, emphasize that the two temporarily become a single divinity who "speaks with one mouth." The Litany of Re calls this dual being "the united one," and a Dynasty 21 papyrus links it with the pair of arms that keep the sun perpetually moving through both the sky and the underworld.

Thus Osiris becomes incorporated into the daily course of the sun, and with him all the blessed dead, since in death they too each become an Osiris. In the Pyramid Texts the name Osiris precedes the king's name as if it were a title; later it is placed before the name of each deceased individual. The sun's journey gives visible proof that light can be reborn in darkness, and the body in death. In the New Kingdom the Egyptians tried to organize and decorate tomb complexes in such a way that the sun would pass through the tomb and thereby lead the deceased, complete with sarcophagus, back onto the path of life.

Life after death does not mean the resumption of life on earth; this new life is in the sky and the underworld. Having become a god, the deceased resides where the gods reside and may encounter them face to face. While still on earth the gods are approached only indirectly, through images and symbols. One such symbol is the sun, but only in the depths of the underworld can humans actually meet the sun in person.

Ramesses II's votive inscription in Abydos to his deceased father, Sety I, describes this meeting with the sun god: "You have entered the sky, you follow the sun god, and are mingled with the moon and stars. Like those who are there, you [also] rest in the underworld beside Osiris, the lord of eternity. Both your arms tow Amun [on his barge] in the sky and in the earth, like the Tireless and Eternal Ones, as you stand at the prow of the sun's ship. As Re appears in the sky your eyes

False-door stela with supplies for eternity for the singer Neferhotep, Dynasty 12. Rijksmuseum van Oudheden, Leiden.

rest on his beauty; when Atum enters the earth you belong to his retinue." Sety I replies: "I am in the underworld, I, your true father, who
has become a god. While I follow the sun I am mingled with the gods,
and I know him [the sun god] who is in his barge."

A scene from the eleventh nocturnal hour in the Book of Gates captures the overpowering moment when the human being views the sun
god. As the face of Re is pulled through the underworld it turns toward the observer—a rare occurrence in Egyptian two-dimensional
art. The frontal position helps emphasize the directness of the visual
contact. The deceased sees the god and knows his secret. He becomes
an initiate, as in the later mystery cults that derive many of their notions from ancient Egyptian concepts of death and the hereafter. But
while in the later period a few select individuals become initiates by
undergoing a symbolic death, in the Pharaonic Period each person enters the realm of the gods and learns the secrets of the afterlife through
his or her actual death. Disseminated and enriched continually by the
Books of the Netherworld, knowledge about the afterlife is no secret
teaching. Although it contains many mysteries, it is not part of a mystery cult; instead, it is a discipline or science that works out an increasing number of details as it continues to develop as a whole.

The journey through the Beyond ends with the morning sunrise.
All of creation celebrates the return of the celestial body, for its rejuvenated appearance gives proof that the depths into which the sun
surrenders itself at night do indeed have regenerative powers. In the

The face of the sun god as he is pulled through
the Netherworld, from the tomb of Ramesses VI,
Valley of the Kings.

Book of Gates, four baboons forcibly open the celestial gate at the end of the nocturnal journey and announce the sun's renewed appearance to the ecstatic world. The sun emerges from the darkness accompanied by eight goddesses who ride on serpents and carry stars in their hands as they praise the sun child. The creation of the world repeats itself, the morning freshness returns: "The sky is gold, the water lapis lazuli, the earth is strewn with turquoise."

At times more somber, skeptical voices speak about the hereafter. After the Amarna Period, for example, laments for the dead and harpists' songs criticize the lavish preparations for the afterlife; the underworld is called the land without light, the land of no return. For all the precise descriptions available, the underworld ultimately remains unknown territory, since "no one returns from there who could describe its condition, report on what is required there, and calm our hearts" (Song of Antef).

The one witness who has entered the underworld and also returned from it each day is the sun. "The essence of darkness reveals itself to whoever looks at the sun," spell 115 of the Book of the Dead says—thus the magical, alien world of the nocturnal sun's light surrenders at least a bit of its mystery. The gate of the horizon opens to reveal the depths of the world: here burns a fire that destroys at the same time it renews, a fire that ignites the sun and infuses it with new brightness. The regenerative powers of the depths are indispensable. All who deliver themselves over to this realm find helping arms. They cannot be destroyed, for the darkness supports them.

CHAPTER 6

THE

TEMPLE

AS

COSMOS

THROUGH the crack of heaven's door it is possible to get a glimpse of the hereafter. On the horizon (*akhet*, or "clearing"), earthly existence comes into contact with the afterlife, and the sun moves from one realm to another; here the deceased finds entry into the world of the dead. When Cheops called his colossal pyramid tomb (2550 B.C.) a "horizon," he gave the first clear evidence of the new worship of the sun that assumed an increasingly dominant role in Egyptian beliefs about the afterlife.

The horizon is associated not only with the sun. All gods have horizons in their temples, where they can establish themselves and appear to the world. The temple—literally "god's house" in Egyptian— is characterized repeatedly as a horizon; it represents the seam

‹ Limestone statue of a queen wearing a wig
overlaid with feathers, circa 1550 B.C. The
Metropolitan Museum of Art, New York.

between this world and the next, peopled by gods and the deceased. The temple is built as a residence for the divinity who is present as a religious image in the inner sanctum; yet it also has a processional path that allows the divinity to venture out into this world and appear to human beings. In addition, the temple mirrors the entire cosmos.

Archaic Period illustrations of shrines show unassuming constructions built of brick, wood, and reed mats rather than stone. Throughout the entire Old Kingdom, in fact, shrines erected for the gods remained modest in terms of both structure and decoration; in contrast, the funerary temples for the pharaohs developed into ever more imposing and elaborately decorated complexes.

With the Middle Kingdom the emphasis shifted, and it becomes possible to speak of decoration in divine temples, as in the charming kiosk built by Senwosret I for Amun-Kamutef in Karnak, or the temple for Renenutet at Medinet Maadi in the Faiyum. An important step in the development of temple architecture was the invention of the pylon, or double tower, that framed the entrance and constituted the exterior temple façade.

In the New Kingdom the axial temple received its definitive shape: pylon, open temple courtyard, column room, offering chamber, barge room, and inner sanctum. The temple itself was built of stone and stood within a high brick wall. The temple complex included priests' living quarters, storerooms, and working quarters; another standard feature was a holy lake within the temple walls. In the Late Period the Egyptians extended the stage for worship to include several different levels by adding shrines on the temple roof as well as subterranean crypts.

In an axial temple each architectural element could be repeated virtually without end; as a result, large temple complexes underwent continuous expansion and never saw completion. The temple of

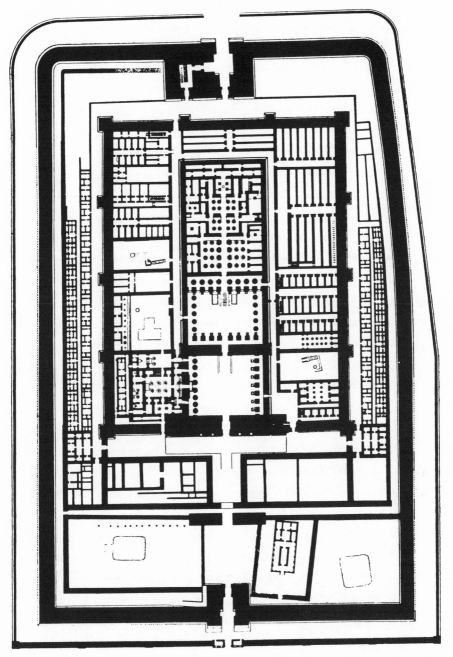

Floor plan of the Medinet Habu temple complex
of Ramesses III.

Amun at Karnak with its ten pylons is an extreme example, but in a considerable number of temples we see at least a doubling of court-yard and pylon. Temple construction provided an ideal opportunity for the Egyptian desire to "extend the existing."

Measurements and proportions of the holy building were by no means arbitrary. The Egyptians preferred cubic measurements divis-ible by ten: the great hypostyle hall at Karnak measures 200 by 100 cu-bits; the pylon of the temple at Medinet Habu is 130 cubits wide, and that of the small Khonsu temple at Karnak 60 cubits wide. At Edfu the temple texts themselves state precise measurements and explain them through mythological references. As at Luxor, the Edfu tem-ple's central axis runs parallel to the Nile, although in general the Egyptians favored an east-west axis, perpendicular to the north-flowing Nile. In certain cases astronomical concerns determined the direction of the central axis: at Abu Simbel and in shrines of Akhena-ton, for example, it is aligned with the course of the sun; in Elephan-tine, the island at Aswan, orientation is provided by Sothis (our Sirius, whose heliacal rising announces the high tide of the Nile).

By ceremonially establishing a temple the Egyptians reenacted cre-ation. Excavation for the temple foundation reached the primordial Nun when it hit ground water. The sacred area was delimited and protected on all sides. Many temples contain illustrations of the foun-dation ritual, particularly the rope-stretching carried out by the king and the goddess Seshat, and the concluding transferal of the house to its master, the main god to be worshipped in the temple. In the Late Period, the ritual of the Opening of the Mouth, which prepared the mouths of statues and mummies so that they might receive nourish-ment and thereby be infused with life, was also performed at the tem-ple in order to "activate" the religious symbols and wall images.

The brick wall enclosing the entire temple area is perforated by a number of stone portals. Its rows of bricks are not in straight lines; they describe something more like a wave, for this wall symbolizes the chaos and primordial water surrounding the ordered area of worship. The temple grows out of and is grounded in Nun; whoever passes through the wall bathes in the primeval water and enters the god's dwelling purified and rejuvenated.

The massive block of the temple itself stands shielded behind additional high walls, which in this inner region are built of stone. New Kingdom and subsequent temple façades consist of a pylon and are usually accessible by interior stairs. On both the pylon and the external walls of the temple, the decoration served an exclusively apotropaic function, that is, it was designed to ward off evil and in particular to frighten enemy forces away from the temple area. The most frequent image is the timeless and generic pharaoh overpowering his enemies. Under Sety I and his successors this gave way to more historical scenes of struggle against specific opponents—Hittites, Syrians, Libyans, and Peoples of the Sea. Hunting scenes also appeared on the pylons, their purpose to keep enemies of every kind from the shrine. Lion-headed water spigots all around the temple served the same protective function.

Colossal statues of the temple's royal client can still be seen standing before many pylons, where they represent the pharaoh's power and influence. While the statues remain, staffs that indicated the presence of divine forces and that were once found in niches in the pylons have disappeared. In both paintings and reliefs, representations of temples show the poles beside the statues, and written texts describe them as reaching to the stars and touching the sky. Most temples show four staffs in front of the pylon. The temple at Karnak, however, had eight; Akhenaton decided that for the large temple of Aton in his new capital, Akhetaten, he would increase the number to ten.

The Luxor temple façade, with pylon, obelisks,
statues, and flagpoles.

Pairs of obelisks, ancient symbols of the sun, likewise occur before
the pylons of divine temples. Solar symbolism and the solar course
held a central place in tombs and temples alike. Evidence dating from
the Ptolemaic Period shows that the Egyptians interpreted the two pylons as Isis and Nephthys, who lift up the sun between them. The motif of the sunrise on the pylon has been traced back to Tutankhamun's
burial treasure, and was used even into the Roman Period, when it appeared on coins. From its first appearance on the horizon, the sun proceeds on its path into the temple interior, where it recurs above every
passageway, primarily in a winged image. The temple may contain
other special rooms or courtyards devoted to sun worship.

When Hatshepsut's architects designed the approach to the temple at Deir el-Bahari as an avenue lined with sphinxes, they introduced an innovation that quickly became the norm. By extending the line of the temple's central axis even beyond the pylon, this avenue design helped indicate the idea of a pathway even more clearly. At the landing are the first guardian figures, which direct one straight toward the narrow passageway in the massive, intimidating pylon towers.

Beyond the entrance pylon lies the large festival courtyard, the "courtyard of the masses." It was not used on a daily basis for worship, but was reserved for large religious festivals that included the public. Here they might glimpse the image of the divinity as priests carried it out of the temple on their shoulders. Presented publicly in this way, the image of the god became directly accessible to the people's requests. To discover the god's wishes they depended on the pronouncements of divine oracles.

In the funerary temple of Ramesses III at Medinet Habu, scenes of the king's triumph dominate the first courtyard. The balcony on the southern wall of the courtyard links the temple and palace; the pharaoh could appear on this balcony as the living image of a divinity and receive the adulation of the assembled crowd. The second courtyard, with its representations of the Min and Sokar festivals, is the actual festival courtyard; here the world of the gods begins and all public aspects of worship come to an end.

The light of the open courtyard gives way to the twilight of the column room, and with the change of light comes a change of scenery. The outward-directed scenes that protect the temple and incorporate it into celebratory processions are replaced by images of worship. At first glance it appears that the same activity recurs everywhere: in varying garb, the king stands praying or making offerings before temple divinities. In theory, every act of worship originates with the king,

Hypostyle hall in the Temple of Amun at Karnak,
built under Ramesses II.

since only the pharaoh can commune with the gods and withstand their powerful influence. The priest who actually fulfills the duties of worship must identify himself before the god as the king's representative: "It is the king who sends me to view the god."

The first impression of a standardized representational scheme should not obscure the fact that the Egyptians carefully selected and arranged the variety of scenes to refer to each other in different ways, and also to reflect the function of the respective rooms in which they appear. Using the key phrase "wall picture and room function," Dieter Arnold has laid the groundwork for understanding these compositions. Derchain, Winter, and other scholars of late temple complexes even speak of a "temple grammar," and try to clarify its syntax and orthography. Not only the scenic arrangement but also the hieroglyphic designations prove important, for in this late phase of Egyptian writing verbal symbols acquired a variety of meanings. To date, interpretative efforts certainly encourage further research, yet they also warn against becoming overly schematic and attempting to account for such details as the different crowns worn by the pharaoh during various activities of worship. In early and very late temples alike, the basic principle of avoiding monotony through variation is a determining factor in pictorial composition.

In the hypostyle hall, the columns are arranged with very little space between them and serve no actual supportive function. The columns, water plants or palms of stone, represent a marsh crossed by a path leading to the inner sanctum. The inner sanctum itself symbolizes the primeval mound of earth that emerged from the marshy waters at the time of creation. For this reason the path that follows the temple's straight central axis leads upward along a gradual incline of steps and ramps; at the same time the ceiling becomes increasingly lower, the rooms darker and narrower. When the Nile overflowed its banks, it flooded the column rooms of many temples, and thereby re-ified the illusion of the primordial swamp.

The Egyptian column always has the form of a plant, whether pa-pyrus, lotus, sedge or palm. During the Ptolemaic and Roman periods the Egyptians used composite capitals that bring together different vegetable elements in ever-changing combinations. These plant col-umns play a dominant role in the basic decoration of the temple and refer to the recurring blessing of the Nile's annual flood, the material basis of all temple worship. The shaft of a column may also be topped by the head of the goddess Hathor or an image of the god Bes as an indication of the building's function. We should keep in mind that col-umns and expanses of wall relief were brightly painted at one time; only in tombs can we still marvel at them in this condition.

The walls of the temple are decorated with clearly ordered scenes from the world of worship. This worship consists of set interactions between humans and gods that make the harmony of the world tan-gible and comprehensible. Worship is the human response to the ex-istence of the gods, a dialogue conducted in both word and deed. Each scene of worship that shows the king presenting offerings to the gods is accompanied by written texts for both parties. These texts describe the pharaoh's action (for example, "donating wine to Hathor, mistress of the sky") as well as the god's promise to the pharaoh, and by exten-sion to all human beings ("To you I give all life, well-being, and health forevermore"). This gift of life may be represented visually in a pic-ture of the divinity extending the sign of life toward the king's nose, or holding a scepter that combines the signs for life, well-being, and duration. As a rule, gods and goddesses appear in complete repose. It is the pharaoh who acts: he prays, makes offerings, rejoices, and even dances before the god.

One particular image in the sanctuary of the temple at Luxor proves more impressive than all other temple scenes in which the pharaoh presents the gods with rich offerings. In this image, the king, Amenophis III, performs no specific act of worship; he merely stands calmly looking at the god. Alone with Amun-Re, he expresses astonishment and piety with the words "Neferwy ubenek,"—How beautiful is your appearance! Awestruck and overwhelmed, the king can only intimate with these words the powerful effect of the divine presence in this innermost chamber of the temple.

The temple that serves as the god's earthly residence should be inviting and encourage the god to stay longer. When he enters the human sphere, the divinity overwhelms with good deeds, the breath of life, and life itself. All the material goods that the pharaoh presented to the god expressed the gratitude of humans to the gods for their presence. Thanksgiving was stated verbally in hymns to various divinities. In the Cairo Hymn to Amun, the creator receives praise "as high as the heaven, as wide as the earth, as deep as the sea" from all his creatures. At festival celebrations this response to the gods' presence was intensified in the scenes of rejoicing, music-making, and dancing on the temple walls.

Worship in Egypt was always official worship. Temples were official institutions that served the state administration, and priests, unless chosen through divine oracles, were appointed by the pharaoh. There was no religious institution separate from the state: the theocracy in Dynasty 21 in which priests also wielded political power was temporary, and only in the Roman and Ptolemaic periods did individual temples gain a strong profile. Resisting foreign domination and evoking their own Egyptian tradition, these later temples belonged to the state administration in a very general sense. Until the early Christian era, the pharaoh remained the basic point of reference both in worship and in the decoration of Egyptian temples. Even as a foreign master,

Macedonian or Roman, he continued to represent the entire human race in dealings with the divine realm; priests fulfilled their assigned duties in the name of the king.

The day-to-day business of worship took place in the darkness of the inner sanctum, supplemented by offering ceremonies in other rooms of the temple building. Those who were not priests might take part in the official forms of worship only during large religious festivals, and even then their participation remained limited. In the Middle Kingdom, however, when the temple acquired greater significance than it had had in the Old Kingdom, priests and officials introduced the custom of placing statues of themselves in the temple. In this way they could enjoy continuous participation—with royal permission, of course—in the temple worship, and profit from prayers and offerings. The Karnak temple complex must have been virtually overrun with such private statuary in the Late Period; the statues were finally removed and buried by the thousands in the famous Karnak cache.

Only higher-ranking officials could afford such temple statues and the direct contact with official worship that they supplied. Others had to rely on the pharaoh as patron to communicate their requests to the gods. If the kingship failed, alternate mediaries—the deceased, who already inhabited the divine world, or sacred animals, considered living images of a divinity—might be invoked. Inconspicuous amulets could also provide the wearer with a sense of both divine benevolence and proximity to the gods.

The difference between the precious religious image guarded by a priest in the inner sanctum and the inexpensive faience figurine worn by a serving woman was a difference of degree only. A comparable distinction existed between the representations on official monuments with the pharaoh standing before the gods, and the testimonies of personal piety on private stelae. The official monuments and religious symbols were for the benefit of all, the private ones for the good of the individual. The god heard not only the priestly hymn of praise, but also the desperate cry of the suffering and the grateful prayer of the redeemed.

State worship was indispensable for the well-being of the entire land. What would happen if it were neglected we learn primarily from texts of the period after Akhenaton's rule. The gods abandoned Egypt and did not return when called; the decaying temples were devoid of divine presence. To avoid such a fate, it was necessary to fill the temple with the life of worship. This meant more than merely decorating the walls; the temple must be filled by the reality of the priests' interaction with the divine image, by the ceremonies of worship conducted within. Such worship might prove quite expensive, since it involved the preparation of offerings, the storage of supplies and instruments of worship, and the procurement of provisions for many employees. Thus the Egyptian temple complex, with its numerous apartments, storehouses, and other attendant buildings, all of brick, also functioned as an economic enterprise. Moreover, the majority of surviving artworks probably came from temple workshops, and written texts were made, copied, and stored in the temple's own "house of life." Temple areas, therefore, were centers for art, literature, and science as well as places of worship.

This bustling temple life is often compared with a physical organism that mirrors the human body in every detail. The temple's symmetrical axis and overall proportions admittedly suggest many points of comparison, but such analogies also hold a great danger in that they may lead us to find correspondences and similarities where the Egyptians themselves saw none. The Egyptians undoubtedly viewed not only religious images but the entire temple building as a physical body that could unite with the psychic *ba* of the god, just as each night the *ba* united with its real body in the underworld. Especially in the Ramesside Period we find temples personified as divine creatures with human forms. The corporeality of the temple is emphasized by the use of gold, bronze, and semi-precious stones such as are recorded in the building inscriptions of Amenophis III. As proven by scrapings taken from temple walls everywhere, the Egyptians believed that helpful, healing powers were at work even in ordinary stone.

The full significance of the material aspect of the temple is perhaps clearest in the practice of incorporating old parts of buildings into newer ones. This practice created a strong sense of historical tradition, a chain whose tight links reached from distant ancestors up to the present. Primarily in Karnak, but in many other places as well, older parts of buildings were torn down first in the course of the rebuilding process. Paradoxically, however, they "survived" in this way, unharmed by the destructive work of stone thieves and lime works. When Amenophis III dismantled the lovely small kiosk of Senwosret I, for example, he incorporated it into his third pylon and thereby saved visual representations and the name of Amun-Kamutef, for whom the kiosk was built, from Akhenaton and later iconoclasts.

The architecture of sacred buildings was determined in part by the fact that the Egyptians did not dedicate individual temples to individual gods. Together with the main divinity in any given sanctuary we find a whole divine community, which in turn necessitated additional shrines or areas of worship, sometimes even separate sanctums within the walls of the larger temple complex. The Anubis and Hathor chapel in the funerary temple of Hatshepsut, and the areas for sun worship found in many temples, exemplify such shrines. The popularity of divine trinities in the New Kingdom resulted in triads of sanctuaries.

The scenes of worship on temple walls give a particularly vivid picture of the variety within the Egyptian pantheon. A text from Edfu describes how the gods enthusiastically unite with the images they find of themselves everywhere in the temple, and in doing so fill the god's dwelling with their presence. Here is the heaven that has been prepared for them in Egypt, and it entices them to prolong their stay. While they travel across the sky in barges, their images remain behind in barge-shaped shrines. In pictures this shrine is always hidden from view, the religious image kept under wraps; nonetheless, the crowned heads of the divinities appear on the prow and stern of the vessel, and in this way become visible, if only in a limited way.

During festival processions the barge would float above the heads of the priests carrying it and reveal itself to the crowd outside the temple. Usually, however, the image rested on a mat that represented the sky. In the temple of Tuthmosis III in Deir el-Bahari, the king appears as the bearer of this sky, and by implication as the support of worship in general. His hands alone touch the sphere of the gods. In the dark inner sanctum behind the barge room, only he—or the priest who represented him—might unlock the shrine. When he broke the seal and removed the lock, he might view the divinity already as a living person.

CHAPTER 7

THE

CONCEPT

OF

MAAT

O<small>NE</small> of the most important scenes of worship found in Egyptian temples depicts the "presentation of Maat." The king presents a divinity with the small figure of a kneeling goddess, identifiable as Maat by the feather she wears on her head. The written texts accompanying the scene, terse as usual, speak only in general terms of the pharaoh's "presentation" or "extension" of Maat. But a hymn that was incorporated into the rituals of Amun and the Opening of the Mouth gives a more detailed explanation of the image. The speaker is the pharaoh, who addresses his words specifically to the sun god: "O Re, Lord of Maat! O Re, who lives in Maat! O Re, who rejoices over Maat! O Re, who loves Maat! O Re, who unites with Maat! . . . I have come to you. I bring you Maat. You live in her. You rejoice

⟨ Funerary mask of a woman, made of cartonnage, paint, gold, faience, and metal, from Thebes, Dynasty 18, circa 1400 B.C. The Metropolitan Museum of Art, New York.

over her. You feed on her. You are strong through her. You endure through her. You are healthy through her. You adorn yourself with her. She casts your foes to the ground. Your heart is glad when you see her! Your fellow gods rejoice when they see Maat in your retinue."

Another, similar hymn has come down to us as part of a daily temple ritual. In this hymn the officiating priest introduces himself as Thoth, the god of wisdom, justice, and moderation, who is often closely associated with Maat. He recites a spell for the presentation of Maat that he performs as the representative of the king. In part he says: "Maat has come so that she may be with you. Maat is present in all your dwellings so that you are furnished with Maat. . . . The robe for your limbs is Maat. . . . Maat is breath for your nose. . . . Maat is your bread, Maat is your beer." As indispensable as food and drink, Maat is a necessity for not only the gods but all creatures. We read in the Book of Gates that even the blessed dead "live in Maat," just as they would be nourished by bread and beer.

Maat is repeatedly described as the "daughter of Re," which makes her the sister of the king who bears the title "son of Re." And indeed, from the time of Amenophis II on, she appears behind the king, just as Isis stands behind the throne of her brother Osiris. After the Amarna Period, Maat occurs also as a winged creature, in keeping with the notion that she provides air and thus enables man to breathe.

According to later texts, Maat is as old as creation but does not predate it. Since creation she has lived among human beings. Having come to them from the gods, she has been entrusted to them, and the human act of presenting Maat returns her to the gods; it thus completes the ritual circle. A text found in Theban tomb number 49 expresses this pattern of give-and-take in an address to Re:

O Re, who created Maat,
Maat is proffered to him.

Sety I presenting Maat, from his temple at Abydos.

Put Maat in my heart,
That I may lead her aloft to your *ka*.
I know that you live in her,
It is you who formed her body.

Some pictures of the presentation of Maat show the goddess twice: once as the offering to the divinity, and again as a figure standing behind him; this indicates that the god has power over her and will continue to exercise it.

Othmar Keel in his fascinating study published in 1974, "Wisdom Plays Before God," discusses many scenes in which Maat as the daughter of the sun god stands before him, amuses him, and jokes with him. Not only did she descend to earth at the time of creation, she is also the favorite child of the creator, and she remains near him and continually entertains him. In making the creator happy she gives pleasure to the entire world. Written texts contain repeated references to rejoicing over Maat; the Coffin Texts instruct Atum to "kiss your daughter Maat, hold her to your nose" (II, 35). In the New Kingdom, comparisons were drawn between Maat and the queen: just as the queen is always at the king's side, Maat remains close by the sun god.

Who is this goddess, Maat, and what does the concept of *maat* that she embodies actually mean? We have mentioned the feather she wears on her head. An ostrich feather may signify the concept of *maat* in representations of the Judgment of the Dead, but in that context it is a strictly phonetic transcription that provides no important information about the essence of *maat*. Of greater significance is a different visual symbol used for *maat*—a beveled pedestal or base on which the throne of a god might stand. From this perspective, *maat* reveals itself as the foundation of all order in the created world; it is the basis for life in a specifically social sense, and in the much broader sense of cosmic order or balance. With this image we begin to realize the timeless applicability of the concept.

For the Egyptians, creation is the positing of *maat*. When Tut-ankhamun reintroduces *maat* in Egypt after Akhenaton's reign, for instance, the land becomes "as it was in the primordial time" imme-diately following creation. The words of admonition of Ipuwer in the First Intermediate Period speak of Maat as spending time with the creator god and the two creative powers Hu, the personification of ut-terance, and Sia, the personification of perception; like them, she ac-companies the god on his nocturnal travels through the underworld. Further, Ptolemaic temple texts speak of Maat's descent to earth and of a paradisiacal primeval time initiated through her.

As texts from the First Intermediate Period and later exhort, to keep *maat* among human beings it is necessary to "do" and "speak" *maat*. Individuals must do what is correct and reasonable, must speak with appropriate words. Passively adapting to a preexisting order, fol-lowing it and respecting it, will not suffice; rather, this order must be established and actively realized time and again. Only through proper behavior and active engagement is world order achieved. With the collapse of the Old Kingdom the Egyptians realized that order was not a given. The first blossoming of Egyptian culture came to an end because the proper thing was no longer done or said.

The concept of *maat* and its personification as a goddess thus played a key role in the Old Kingdom, albeit primarily in individual names and titles. Nonetheless, we see that the concept extends back to the very beginning of Egyptian history. In the Pyramid Texts *maat* stands intimately linked with the sun god; at the same time, the de-ceased king also emphasizes that he has spoken *maat*, or has replaced injustice with *maat*.

The first clear indications that injustice has driven out *maat* occur in the "Literature of Despair" of the First Intermediate Period and Middle Kingdom. No longer assumed as a given, *maat* must now be won through a struggle against powerful forces. *Maat* is as necessary as the air people breathe: "It is breath for the nose to do *maat*," says the Eloquent Peasant in his third lament. Addressed to the administrator Rensi, the lament praises him as the one "who destroys lies and allows *maat* to develop." Writers during this time raised their voices against lying and vile behavior in general. The same Eloquent Peasant, cites in the eighth lament "the marvelous word that issued from the mouth of the sun god himself: 'Speak *maat* and practice *maat*, for she is great, mighty and lasting.' " In the same lament we learn that Maat "remains until eternity. She accompanies the person who practices *maat* down into the realm of death. He is placed in a coffin and buried with her; his name shall not be erased from the earth."

Terms contrasting with *maat* are *isfet*, whose specific meaning is unclear but whose connotations include injustice or wrong, disorder, and unreasonableness; *gereg*, or "lie"; and *khab*, "the crooked." Against these terms of opposition, *maat* may be interpreted as truth, justice, authenticity, correctness, order, and straightness. It is the norm that should govern all actions, the standard by which all deeds should be measured or judged. Even so, in keeping with Egyptian ethics, *maat* is a norm that should not become an overly rigid standard or model of behavior. The Eloquent Peasant text contains a vivid warning neither to scrimp when filling *maat* nor to let it overflow (sixth lament), and in his teaching Ptahhotep commands: "Adhere to *maat*, but do not exaggerate."

The universal sense of the term *maat* has no precise equivalent in any other language; perhaps the Sanskrit word *rta* comes closest. Contemporary translations have consistently yielded lengthier, more detailed definitions. H. Bonnet, for example, understands *maat* as "correctness" in the sense of an immanent lawfulness not only in the natural and social order, but also in the sacred order, since the "presentation of Maat" motif epitomizes all worship activities. S. Morenz sur-

Two *ba* souls offering incense to Amenet, goddess of the West. Interior of the innermost lid of the coffins of Henettowy, from Thebes, Dynasty 21. Metropolitan Museum of Art, New York.

mises that the term initially referred only to physical "straightness" or "evenness," and over time became laden with more complex meanings. W. Westendorf interprets the verb *maa* as "to give things a direction," a definition that assigns *maat* the role of "leader" or "direction giver." R. Anthes writes about *maat* in the Amarna Period but his words are applicable to other periods as well: "Maat holds this small world together and makes it into a constitutive part of world order. She is the bringing home of the harvest; she is human integrity in thought, word, and deed; she is the loyal leadership of government; she is the prayer and offering of the king to the god. Maat encompasses all of creation, human beings, the king, the god; she permeates the economy, the administration, religious services, the law. All flows together in a single point of convergence: the king. He lives in Maat and passes her on, not only to the sun god above but also to his subjects below."

While the Egyptians themselves have given us no definition of *maat* per se, they of course knew what it was, and were firmly convinced that it could be taught: not through the transmission of definitions, but through teaching and living an exemplary life—in short, through the realization of *maat*. This is the goal of the Egyptian "wisdom literature," or more accurately, "life instructions." We possess a considerable number of these popular texts, which date from as early as the Old Kingdom and as late as the Roman Period, since they were widely distributed and were copied over and over in schools. In the earlier periods their practical goal was to establish guidelines for correct behavior in specific situations: on the street, in a public dispute, before a magistrate, as a houseguest, in one's own household, and in dealing with one's wife, superiors, friends, or servants. Royal instructions might even address proper political action, but in general the texts remained on the level of etiquette books concerned primarily with customs and common practices. Knowledge of *maat* is continually being reformed and reactualized. Whoever has no knowledge can neither recognize nor practice *maat*, and only by hearing and obeying is it possible to acquire such knowledge.

In the Ramesside Period, however, the Egyptians began to doubt the possibility of teaching or conveying *maat* through wisdom. The dialogue that concludes the Instruction of Ani expresses these doubts by linking *maat* with the capricious will of the god, and the Instruction of Amenemope refers to Maat as "the great burden of the god. He gives her to whomever he wishes." Human beings, in other words, no longer have any influence. The anonymous god mentioned in this text in all probability is the sun god as creator, since he is one of the few divinities to whom Maat can be proffered. In the great pillared hall at Karnak she is offered only to Amun, Re-Harakhty, and Ptah, the three gods of the imperial triad who replace Akhenaton's single god, Aton. It is also possible to present Maat to Thoth, guardian of all lawful order; she is considered his spouse and his successor in the first divine dynasty. But it would be inconceivable to present Maat to either Seth or Mont, the war god. Maat is equated with only one goddess, Tefnut, the first goddess to emerge from Atum and who, like Maat, came into existence at the time of creation.

Quite early on, individual names testify to the religious significance of Maat, and in the New Kingdom numerous temples were dedicated to the goddess. These temples had their own priesthood and their own special herds of cattle, complete with a "cattle master of Maat." Despite the existence of a cult devoted specifically to her, Maat's general religious importance, as expressed in the presentation of Maat, is incomparably greater. Each person who appeared before a divinity had to possess religious purity as well as harmony with Maat; the same was true for every deceased person who faced a trial in the hereafter.

The act of offering an image of Maat to the gods represented the individual's contribution toward making *maat* more complete in the world. Only the king who employed *maat* against foreign enemies could realize it in a historico-political sense. In the more mundane realm of everyday life, each person was responsible for doing and speaking *maat* in order to increase and secure its presence. In the Ramesside Period the presentation scene was no longer the exclusive province of royalty; officials too are depicted presenting Maat. It should be noted, however, that such images have been documented only in now inaccessible subterranean Theban burial chambers, which in all likelihood were themselves modeled after royal tombs.

With the notion of *maat* the Egyptians developed a universal concept that could serve as the foundation for any and every type of order, whether in nature or in the human sphere. In a very general sense *maat* applied also to music, poetry, and art. It was the harmony of tones, the melodious sound, the proper measure in architecture, and the antidote for every form of excess. Measuring, weighing, and counting likewise stood intimately linked with *maat*. We have no evidence that the term had a different, more specific meaning at the beginning of history. From the start it occurs in the broadest imaginable sense and refers to the social and natural order alike, to every product of the creator god and of human beings. The radical changes of the First Intermediate Period doubtless contributed to a revised conception of *maat*, which took the form of an increased emphasis on its social application and on the administration of justice.

Maat must have been associated with the dispensation of justice as early as Dynasty 5, because the vizier, the highest legal official then, was called "the priest of Maat." And in the Instructions for the vizier noted earlier, we read: "You will be successful in your position if you do *maat*. The vizier has been [Maat's] guardian since the dawn of time."

King Haremheb in Dynasty 18 issued decrees containing quite specific punishments in the name of *maat*, "in order to ward off *isfet* and destroy *gereg*." In court decisions the defendant was not declared guilty or innocent; rather, one of the opposing parties was correct (*maa*), and the other incorrect. In this way the Egyptian judge sought to avoid assigning guilt; he preferred to find a balance acceptable to both parties before the court. As a legal concept, *maat* subsumes all other terms such as "law" and "divine decree"; ultimately it is synonymous with the law itself. The term also retains a universal scope in the context of the death tribunal, where the essence of the individual comes face to face with *maat*.

Understood as a general sense of justice, *maat* involves the protection of the socially underprivileged and the achievement of balance between ownership and poverty. The biographies of officials, left in their tombs and intended to present ideal images and attest to their lasting accomplishments in life, emphasize repeatedly: "I gave bread to the hungry, water to the thirsty, clothing to the naked, a ferry to those who had no boat." The more responsibility an individual bears for the general welfare, the greater his or her responsibility to practice *maat*. Because of his political stature, the pharaoh was the one who brought *maat* and chased away *isfet*, and who could assert: "I have brought *maat* into this land where there was none"; "I have introduced *maat* throughout the lands, and stabbed *isfet* to the ground."

The teachings that disseminate knowledge about *maat* do not concentrate solely on heads of state and administrators. Royal teachings from Dynasties 10 and 12 represent the exception rather than the rule. It was of utmost importance that even the petty official have an image of Maat in his workplace that he could use as a rule of conduct. In files of the Ramesside Period we see all too clearly how much reality diverges from the ideal, and how administrative circles are rife with embezzlement, manipulation, and bribery. Against this historical background, the pharaoh's claim to have brought *maat* into a land where it did not exist before acquires a particularly timely significance. In the accusations made against the foreman Paneb, who supervised the workers in the tombs of the Valley of the Kings under King Siptah, which are preserved in a document in the British Museum, and in the "Elephantine scandal" under Ramesses IV and V, we find a dramatic picture of actual conditions. In short, the individuals concerned appear to have been completely ignorant of *maat*. Like the Old Kingdom that preceded it, the New Kingdom met its ultimate destruction for lack of *maat*.

Nevertheless, such experiences did not lead to an attitude of resignation. The Egyptians learned instead to appreciate *maat* as the hope for another chance. Although Maat may have been driven out, she could return thanks to the assiduous work of the ruler or the individual. In this sense *maat* resembled the eye of Horus, wounded time and time again and subsequently healed. Both symbolized a constantly endangered order that must repeatedly be established anew.

The presentation of the eye of Horus, or *udjat* eye, by the pharaoh or priest had the same basic significance as the presentation of Maat. The gesture gave visible proof that all disruptions and threats to order had been removed, and that justice and harmony ruled once more. On two statues we find the symbols explicitly joined in the inscription: "My arms carry the *udjat* eye, I present *maat*." The sacred eye is often shown in the hands of a baboon—an allusion to Thoth, who healed the eye, brought about reconciliation, and in turn reestablished *maat*. Thoth also bears the responsibility for *maat* in his role as judge and vizier of the gods. Further, as a lunar god he is a connection to the world of the stars: the wounded-then-healed eye he proffers represents the waxing and waning of the moon. When in the form of a baboon Thoth crouches in the sun god's barge and extends the eye to Re, he indicates the cosmic order of the stars, which unwaveringly follow their course. This too is *maat*.

Egyptian texts state that while evil, injustice, and irrationality may enjoy temporary success, experience shows that ultimately they will find no secure harbor. These forces have no permanence, and because they bring no lasting profit, they are useless and dangerous. It was difficult, even impossible, to realize *maat* over an extended period of time, at least in this life. Yet the Old Kingdom vizier Ptahhotep asserts in his Instructions that "if the end has come, *maat* remains." "The man who is in harmony with *maat* will endure"; only by doing *maat* is it possible to safeguard one's tomb and continued existence after death.

Maat is that which remains in the end. At the same time, it did not represent a utopia for the Egyptians, as social utopias were utterly foreign to their realistic, pragmatic sensibilities. As a guiding principle *maat* is a point of orientation or a standard of measurement; it is the "ought" against which the "is" of life is ruthlessly and repeatedly measured and almost always found lacking. The scene of the offering of Maat shows the constant exertion required to increase the amount of *maat* throughout the world, since, as the sixth lament of the Eloquent Peasant says:

Whoever decreases lying promotes *maat*,
Whoever supports good reduces evil to nothing,
As satiety drives away hunger,
Clothing covers nakedness,
As the sky becomes clear after a violent storm,
. . . as fire cooks raw food,
As water slakes thirst.

In this notion of continuous striving lies both the relevance and the pragmatic meaning of the term *maat*. It does not imply the complete elimination of lies, irrationality, and meanness from the world, since

Papyrus of Ty, showing the weighing of the heart
against the feather of Maat, from a Dynasty 21
tomb at Deir el-Bahari. The Metropolitan Museum
of Art, New York.

these will exist as long as humans do; they are part of human frailty, a
condition that becomes only more pronounced in our world of tech-
nological perfection. Human beings can do almost anything, but they
cannot change. In view of this reality, the Egyptians developed their
modest ideal of increasing *maat*. In more contemporary terms, the
ideal might be expressed as follows: Whoever reduces the destruction
of the environment, even in a very limited way, helps promote survival
and improve the quality of life; whoever does so increases rather than
decreases *maat*.

Contemporary society has seen numerous ethical role models set up only to be discarded later. Whether we speak of maximizing profit or of solidarity, of rightist or leftist utopias, of the welfare state or of a state under the rule of law, the problem of "justice for all" is not yet solved. *Maat*, however, proves a reliable guiding principle that can help approach this goal. *Maat* cannot eliminate social differences, nor does it aim to, but it does impose obligations on all social classes. Rather than serve the interests of a single group, it extends beyond the social order to include all living creatures and all of nature. *Maat* has close ties to the Egyptian sense of measure and balance. *Maat* is a moderate path that avoids extremes.

A minimum of prosperity is required to attain *maat*. According to the Instruction of King Merikare, "a poor man does not speak according to *maat*"; survival is the sole concern of the indigent. Yet *maat* does not necessarily aim to increase prosperity and profit; it contains a warning against all forms of excess, and greed in particular comes under repeated attack as a fundamental evil in Egyptian life teachings. *Maat* strives for the just distribution and fair use of all that is available. It corresponds in large part to what we might call action governed by reason and foresight.

Faced with the virtually limitless possibilities and countless temptations of the modern world, rational human beings seem to find it increasingly difficult to resist senseless consumption and to renounce profits made only at another's expense. By recalling the principle of *maat*, we may begin to find this necessary renunciation more tolerable and sensible; we may recognize that it too belongs to the order of the world. Whoever proffers Maat and follows Maat, whoever keeps an eye fixed steadily on this goddess, cannot go wrong.

CHAPTER 8

H I S T O R Y

A S

C E L E B R A T I O N

Since time and space define all existence, existence, according to Heidegger, should be understood as essentially historical. However, against the background of this generous idea of history, a more particular understanding of the term results when humans select from a vast multitude of events and record these selections. Compared with the millions of years of natural history and evolution, this type of thinking in historical categories is a recent development. Its fundamental characteristics emerge clearly for the first time in Egyptian monuments dating from around 3000 B.C.

Early Egyptian works of art provide some sense of the prehistoric world view, but they do not record events we would call truly historical. Hunting and battle scenes depict events not yet structured in terms of a specific time and place. In a world ruled by unpredictable forces that are sometimes allied with and at other times opposed to one another, these events follow no grand design, no master plan. With the introduction of writing, however, it does become possible to order and denote individual happenings, and record them as history.

The first distinct historical Egyptian monuments are connected with a king by the name of Scorpion, who ruled over Upper Egypt and areas of the Nile delta prior to Dynasty 1, sometime around 3000 B.C. A fragment of the ceremonial Libyan Palette, now in the Egyptian Museum in Cairo, focuses on a single incident and thereby separates it from the static generality of battle and worship. A few written characters suffice to indicate a historical consciousness. One records the king's name and thus assigns the monument to the time of his rule. A second, a throwing stick placed above the oval symbol of the earth, forms the name Tjehenu, denoting Libya and the regions west of the

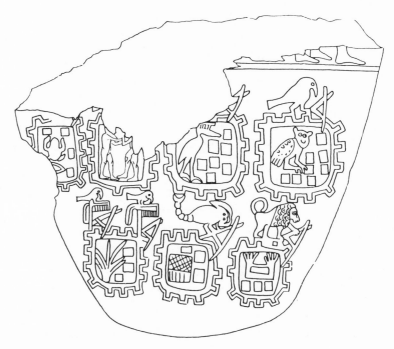

Detail of the Libyan Palette. Cairo Museum.

Nile delta. On the other side of the palette are carefully ordered rows of seven fortified towns, each of which is named with a hieroglyph referring to Buto, the capital of Lower Egypt in the western delta. Crowned by animal figures grasping hoes, the towns probably represent different aspects of royal or divine power. Arranged on a base line above the towns are partially visible feet.

The historical message conveyed by these simple means might be rendered as follows: "King Scorpion conquered an important area of the western delta and thereby brought in much booty." Our inability to date the event any more specifically, to assign it a day or even a year in keeping with our own practices of measuring time, by no means lessens the historicity of the event itself. In ancient Oriental historical records, a given time was generally indicated by the name of the king alone. A certain multiplicity of meanings characterizes these oldest and, to our way of thinking, all too condensed bits of historical information; only over time do they become more specific and comprehensive. Even in the case of the Libyan Palette the details do not make certain whether the event recorded is the conquest or the founding of a city, and scholars continue to debate whether the forces depicted in animal form refer to divinities or to the king.

Approximately a generation later the growing historical consciousness of the Egyptians finds vivid expression in the Palette of King Narmer. Also in the Egyptian Museum in Cairo, the palette was originally a votive offering in the temple of Hieraconpolis.

On the reverse side, the king raises a club to kill an enemy who has already sunk to the ground. This typical scene of the "smiting of the foes" occurs in prehistory and remains basically unchanged into the Roman Period. The oldest known example comes from a prehistoric tomb painting from Hieraconpolis, in which a male figure, certainly a chieftain, stands at the edge of the swirling, surging mass of discon-

Detail of the Battlefield Palette from Abydos,
circa 3170 B.C., commemorating the defeat of a
Libyan people. A lion, who probably represents
the king, ravages the corpses on the battlefield.
British Museum, London.

nected world events. Having captured three bound foes—the hieroglyphic equivalent of "many"—the man beats them with a raised
club. Although the painting may narrate an actual occurrence, it does
not yet concern a historical event in the narrow sense of the term. The
hunting and battle scenes, the motifs of alliances of power, and the
smiting of the enemies are timeless images; they are symbols of world
events like those found in myth.

On the Palette of Narmer the same basic scene gives a dramatically
different impression, involving a higher degree of aesthetic sophistication. Narmer is probably the legendary King Menes, who conquered the peoples of northern Egypt and united the two parts of

Egypt under a central rule, which lasted, with brief interruptions, until the time of Alexander the Great. The Palette of Narmer depicts this conquest of the northwest delta. On the front the king wears the tall crown of Upper Egypt and on the reverse the newly won crown of Lower Egypt. The accompanying texts, in hieroglyphs, remove the depicted action from the timelessness of myth and introduce it into history. Now it is a particular King X who, in a specific year of his reign, conquers a specific enemy Y.

Another example may help illustrate how, in the awakening historical consciousness of Egypt, mythical generality gradually gave way to historical particularity. The earliest Egyptian kings all bear the single title Horus, which indicates their status as the earthly incarnation of the falcon-featured celestial god. The title also appears as a mark of ownership on several objects from the end of the prehistoric period, although no specific king's name occurs in this connection. The written symbol for the Horus title consists of a rectangular shape suggesting the floor plan of the palace complex; inside the rectangle is a frontal view of the palace façade with its gates and niches. The Horus falcon appears above the rectangle; according to the conventions of Egyptian sign arrangement, Horus is inside, not above, the palace. Interpreted as "Horus in the palace," the sign is a manifestation of the god and thus of a mythical entity.

King Scorpion writes his name in the area between the falcon and the palace façade, and thereby describes himself as "Horus Scorpion." As a result of this initiative, Scorpion and his successors emerge from prehistoric anonymity, and the god becomes a specific Horus, a Horus X, who in the person of the reigning pharaoh plays a role in the historical world of spatial and temporal particulars. Just as the god Horus will always exist, so too will the "Horus in the palace," the king. But unlike the god, Horus Scorpion and Horus Narmer are historical entities, who exist only once, as indicated in inscriptions of later pharaohs that speak of a king "who in all eternity will not be repeated."

Egyptian historical records attest to a keen awareness that individual people and events are unique. In some cases we find admissions of failings or shortcomings on the part of the pharaoh, who was usually considered infallible. Even so, the overall historical picture yielded by official inscriptions and pictures is heavily determined by recurring, typical events. In the decorative relief of the Palette of Narmer and other early monuments, the players change but their basic roles remain constant: as defender of world order, the king consistently appears as an indefatigable fighter and conqueror of his foes; the set role of the god is to place the enemy "under [the pharaoh's] soles"; the official always stands in the background, loyal and at the ready; and the enemy invariably loses and must beg for the king's mercy.

Even when the reality of the situation was, according to our own criteria, completely different, official historical records describe the events by using the same basic scenario with the same assigned roles. In May 1274 B.C. Ramesses II and one of his four legions were ambushed by the Hittites and their allies near the Syrian city of Kadesh on the Orontes. The Egyptians narrowly escaped catastrophe, and were pursued by their enemies even after retreating from the field as beaten men. Ramesses II recorded this battle in all the important temples of Egypt and Nubia, and initiated a peace policy that later culminated in an alliance between the two great powers. But we will never be entirely sure just how that fateful day unfolded.

The records of historical events have three components: the events themselves, which furnish both the framework of the action and a series of individual details; a political aim that determines particular accents; and an underlying sense of history that provides a fundamental pattern for rendering the events. With this pattern, all those involved

Palette of Narmer. Cairo Museum.

play set roles much as they would in a religious drama. "Like scare-
crows in their numbers," the enemy proves impressive by virtue of size
but ultimately falls powerless under the hooves of the king's charging
horses. The pharaoh is the sun who dispels the forces of darkness
wherever he appears, and even the failure of his army does not have a
strictly political emphasis. Rather, it serves as a backdrop for the bril-
liant accomplishments of the powerful pharaoh and his god, Amun.
One text describes this pairing of pharoah and god as more effective
than "millions of foot soldiers, hundreds of thousands of charioteers,
and ten thousand brothers and children standing together as one
man."

History is stylized but not falsified in ancient Egypt. It resembles
religious worship in that it too is celebrated in firmly established rituals. Historical inscriptions and images from ancient Egypt do not
narrate actual events. Instead they provide entry into a solemn, ritualistic world that contains no chance or random elements. The Egyptians had no historiography as we know it, no objective narrative of
the past. In their view the past was of interest only to the extent that it
was also the present and could be the future.

Although Pepy II (ca. 2254–2160 B.C.) probably never waged a campaign against the Libyans himself, he had artists make a careful, detailed copy of a picture showing a victory over the Libyans that had
taken place two centuries before, at the time of his predecessor Sa-
hure. The same ancient image was copied by artists under the Ethio-
pian King Taharka (690–664 B.C.). In a similar vein, Tutankhamun,
who died when he was probably no more than eighteen years old, was
presented as the victor over Africans and Asians he most certainly
never fought. And following the example of Ramesses II, Ramesses
III (1184–1153 B.C.) had his own funerary temple at Medinet Habu
decorated with the same scenes of the battle against the Hittites at Ka-

desh that Ramesses II had used in his Ramesseum, despite the fact that in the meantime the Hittites, the former foe of Egypt, had disappeared completely from the political scene.

In this and many other cases the exact recording of historical events proves far less important than the suggestion of a ritual reenactment. This is even more evident in the *sed* festival, the royal celebration of renewal, which has been documented from the Archaic Period through the Ptolemaic Period. In the course of a generation the pharaoh exhausted his powers, so that after thirty years' rule he needed to undergo a ritual regeneration in the form of the *sed* festival. Only a few kings reigned long enough to celebrate this festival and record it. Nonetheless, visual images and references to the festival belong to the fixed decorative scheme of royal buildings. The festival thus became immortalized even when it served as an idealized goal but never took place. Which *sed* festivals actually occurred cannot always be ascertained.

In the temples of the Old Kingdom, scenes of worship appear alongside scenes of battle and hunting; many parallel images show that the hunt and battle were interchangeable. The pharaoh triumphed over enemy forces and kept them at a distance from the sacred area of the temple; correspondingly, bloody animal sacrifice in the temple signified a ritualistic suppression of the mythical enemies of the gods. The role of the mythical foe can be assumed also by political enemies, as we see in the practice of offering prisoners or booty from a military campaign to the divinity. Blurring the distinction between worship and history in a similar way at Medinet Habu, Ramesses III depicted the ahistorical battle with the Hittites side by side with his actual triumphs over the Libyans and Sea Peoples. On the back of the southern pylon tower are hunting scenes with wild oxen and wild asses, counterparts of the battle scenes. In the earlier Rames-

seum of Ramesses II, discussed above, the timeless smiting of the foes
was replaced with historical images of the battle at Kadesh on the pylon towers. The purpose of using an actual event did not differ from
that of using the more general theme. In both cases the scenes served
an apotropaic function; they warded off evil and frightened away enemies who might otherwise threaten the holy spot.

The Egyptians' attitudes toward the spoken word and the pre-
scribed ritualistic act were comparable. By recording words and acts
in tombs and temples, they gave them permanence and increased their
effectiveness: on temple walls the pharaoh continues to triumph over
peoples who have long since disappeared, and to celebrate festivals for
gods in whom no one believes. What these images and written texts
contain in the way of historical information can be determined only
through a critical analysis that takes into account fundamental differences between the Egyptian conception of history and our own.

The ideal of the pharaoh as a creator who proves himself through
buildings and other monuments could shape historical reality. Ramesses II, for instance, reigned for sixty-six years, but inscriptions on at
least three of his major buildings date from his first year of rule. After
ascending the throne he apparently began immediate construction on
a number of colossal temples: Abydos, Abu Simbel, the Ramesseum,
as well as the pylon of the temple at Luxor; in addition, he completed
the great hypostyle hall at Karnak and oversaw the construction of a
massive tomb complex in the Valley of the Kings. Such a tremendous
exertion of energy at the beginning of a new pharaoh's reign makes
sense only in terms of the Egyptian conception of history, and resulted
in an astonishing wealth of monuments from even relatively short periods of rule.

The concept of history that in these cases has a direct impact on
reality reveals more than surface parallels with the realm of worship

and ritual. In ancient Egypt, history was a religious drama in which all of humanity participated. It was an intensification of the great festivals in which ritual performance left the privacy of the temple sanctuary and entered the public domain. Because there was an essential link between the two activities, it is no coincidence that historical battle images and large-scale festival scenes began to appear in temple decoration at the same time. From the earliest annals on, the elaborate festivals and their celebration by the king were recorded as historic events.

Thus, we might characterize the ancient Egyptian sense of history with the phrase "history as celebration." The description has provoked some controversy, since, as a shorthand expression, it cannot do justice to all aspects of the Egyptian view. Of concern here, however, is the basic tone sounded again and again in ancient Egypt, the ceremonial character of history, which exists in many other cultures as well, even to the present day.

According to this view, history is played out in the form of a fixed ritual in accordance with the Annals. Begun in about 2900 B.C., the Annals describe as well as prescribe, and they address not only what has happened in the past, but also what happens in the present and what will happen again in the future. As texts concerning religious rites and practices, the Annals are solemnly fixed at the beginning of each period of rule together with the new king's title and program of government. A basic pattern is established for what should occur under the new government, and the future is rendered as familiar as the past.

The Egyptians began writing annals at the beginning of historical time. From the reign of King Aha in Dynasty I, the texts identified or named individual years of the king's reign, as these were not yet counted consecutively. We find headings such as "Defeat of the Asiatics," "Festival of the Horus-Star-of-the-Gods," "Forming the Khen-tamenti Statue," and "Shooting of the Hippopotamus" on small wooden or ivory tablets used as labels for oil jars; later the names were incised on the containers themselves. In the ancient Near East the practice of naming years after single events or several different events lasted even longer than in Egypt, where a transition occurred in the early Old Kingdom. Although it was still possible to use an expression like "the year of eating hyenas [out of hunger]," by 2600 B.C. the Egyptians began to write official dates that corresponded to the regular levying of taxes, and later to the years of a pharaoh's rule.

In the latter system counting started over with each change of government, and thereby resulted in cyclical recurrence rather than a unilinear progression of dates. Each king began time anew. Even as he marked a new start, however, he repeated what had occurred before

Annals tablets of King Dewen.

in much the same way that existence in the hereafter was believed to repeat life on earth—yet another reminder that to the Egyptians man did not move along a straight line through time.

The old names of years were grouped according to periods of rule and summarized in lists. None of the original lists remain, but we do have fragments of copies on stone that were made in the Late Period and placed in temples. One such record, the Annals Stone, now in Palermo, encompassed the entire early historical period up to Dynasty 5. On this stone the fields indicating individual years are arranged in horizontal rows; as time progressed, the number of events recorded each year increased.

The occurrences recorded on the Annals Stone fall into several basic categories: the modeling of statues; the construction of worship complexes; the celebration of national festivals; the commencement of new governments, and festivals of renewal; the defeat of enemies, and ritual hunts; and the annual Nile floods, which determined both the fertility of the land and the taxes levied in a given year. These set events recurred with monotonous regularity. Occasionally, their cyclical character received further emphasis through the addition of an ordinal number in notations such as "first defeat of the East" or "second time for the Sokar festival."

The standardization of occurrences through selection and repetition characterizes not only the Annals in particular, but the official Egyptian recording of history in general. An exemplary instance is found in the description of the battle of Megiddo (1458 B.C.), where Tuthmosis III defeated a dangerous coalition of Asiatic princes. The Royal Annals, which are actually excerpts from the king's wartime journal, dispense with the battle in the following brief lines: "His Majesty became powerful against them there at the head of his army. Whereupon they saw how His Majesty became powerful against them, and fled in great disarray to Megiddo, their faces panic-stricken." Other details from the course of the war are described at greater length, and some two centuries later we find a wealth of information in Ramesses II's account of the battle of Kadesh. While the typicality of the event may stand in the foreground, it does not necessarily result in a strictly deterministic view of history. Something completely new may happen at any time, "to the astonishment of the entire land." A popular expression in royal inscriptions was: "Never since the primeval time did such a thing happen," and especially the kings of the New Kingdom liked to boast of their achievements by saying that they had found nothing comparable in the Annals. Such claims recall the dynamic principle discussed in chapter 4: the extension of the existing, which manifests itself in the will to surpass the achievements of one's predecessors.

The Annals and royal inscriptions usually do not name Egyptian officials, so to make their acquaintance we need to seek them out in their own tombs or in documents that have survived by chance. In ancient Egypt, more than in any other culture, a person's tomb was considered a memorial to his or her life. Tomb inscriptions were addressed to future generations "who will follow . . . in millions of years," as indicated in the tomb of a Ramesside steward in Memphis. The key information follows immediately: "I let you know how respected I was by His Majesty." Biographies preserved in tombs dating back to the early Old Kingdom do not attempt to chronicle an individual's life. They focus instead on the accomplishments and status of the deceased, whose rank depended on both closeness to the pharaoh and the successful completion of royal commissions. In the tomb, biography, rank, and achievement find a permanent record.

While some biographies stress the active participation of officials in royal battles and construction projects, others use the words "I

Two emaciated desert nomads on a late Dynasty 5 relief from King Unas's funerary monument at Saqqara provide a rare reference to a historical event. Musée du Louvre, Paris.

saw . . ." to suggest that they participated as spectators. The biography of Inene, mayor of Thebes and architect for a number of Dynasty 18 kings, describes his role as viewer thus: "I saw the great monuments he [Amenophis I] built in Karnak. . . . I saw how both large obelisks were erected. . . . I saw how the sublime ship was built. . . . I saw how the rock tomb of His Majesty [Tuthmosis I] was carved out in isolation, unseen and unheard."

In the religious drama of history the only real players are the pharaoh and his enemies. The king is ubiquitous in the countless scenes of worship on temple walls, since he alone may come face to face with the gods. The pharaoh dominates the scenes of the large official festivals as well. The Egyptian concept of royalty is quite sophisticated in the balance it strikes between human and divine components. While the king is human, it is "impossible to distinguish" him from the gods, as we read on one of the shrines of Tutankhamun. The formerly popular designation "god king" is too simplistic and therefore misleading. For example, the birth legend recorded in picture cycles primarily under Hatshepsut and Amenophis III identifies the king as the son of a divine father (Amun) and human mother (the queen). Another indication of the pharaoh's status as son of a god occurs in the title "son of Re," which the king bore as early as Dynasty 4. Divine and human elements are joined in his parentage; he resembles the gods without being one; he is the earthly, visible image of a god and assumes a divine role on earth.

The god he plays is the sun god Re, creator of the world. Since the beginning of the Middle Kingdom, the Egyptians devised various epithets referring to the sunlike character of the king. He was called the one "who illuminates the Two Lands," "sun of human beings, who drives darkness from Egypt," and even more explicit, "Re of foreign countries," "Egypt's Re," and "sun of rulers." New Kingdom officials called out to him "You are Re!" and Amenophis III, Tutankhamun, and the Ramesside kings gave visual expression to the idea of the king's essential equality with Re by placing their own names inside the solar disk.

Just as the sun dispels the powers of darkness when it appears, the pharaoh conquers the enemies of Egypt through his appearance alone. His rays are the arrows that upon leaving his bow never miss their mark as he charges forth in his chariot. And just as each sunrise makes the world visible once more, the pharaoh illuminates the world with monuments and buildings whose sunlike glow floods Egypt. The shining colors of temple reliefs, the gilt on individual parts of buildings, and the high gloss of precious stones in statues all contribute to this luminous splendor. They create a heaven on earth, a heaven whose sun is the king.

The royal privilege of constructing monuments proved the pharaoh's ability to repeat what the creator god had done at the beginning of time. The pharaoh's deeds allowed the breath that stirred at the creation of the world to be felt once more. For the Egyptians, that creation was not a onetime occurrence; it needed continual repetition and regeneration. Each new government signaled a new beginning for the world, and before its commencement primeval chaos reigned, as documented in Egyptian texts that report anarchy at the death of the ruler. Injustice and disorder would rule until a new king could ascend the throne and reintroduce *maat* as the basis of all order. Laughter and rejoicing would then take the place of sorrow, and the lawlessness of anarchy would give way to a spirit of peace and reconciliation in which a person might even "embrace the man who killed his father."

All this has little to do with historical reality, as a true interregnum existed only rarely between governments or dynasties in Egypt. Even in the face of frequent disappointment, however, the hope that a new government would bring improvement and renewal was still cherished, as it is today. In his role as creator, the pharaoh transformed disorder into order, and chaos into structure, with himself at its center. The regularity with which the moon went through its phases and Nile floods renewed the earth reconfirmed the Egyptian conviction that in nature and in history alike, exemplary patterns determined the course of events. One could depend on the recurrence of such events, yet also know that each time they recurred the specifics would be different; repetition did not mean the eternal recurrence of the same.

The sense of history that informed the Pharaonic Period remained alive as long as ancient Egyptian culture did. Only with the advent of Christianity did the pharaoh as creator god become dispensable and the course of history point toward a new goal. As Tutankhamun wrote in the inscription on the "restoration stela" that marked the end of the turmoil of the Amarna Period, the goal of pharaonic history is "that the world become as it was at the time of creation." In other words, working toward the future is actually striving toward the furthest imaginable point in the past: the moment when the world began. Once again we see time assume the circular form of the ouroboros, the snake that bites its own tail. The historical work of the pharaoh and his assistants aims to restore to the world something of the perfection it enjoyed at the time of its origin.

CHAPTER 9

BODY

AND

SOUL

EGYPTIAN ideas about the body and its impor-
tance are well exemplified by their burial rituals, particularly the custom of mummification. They developed this practice early in the Old
Kingdom, around the time of the first stepped pyramids, so that
they might preserve the human form, complete with hair and skin
(albeit somewhat shriveled and darkened), beyond death. The art of
mummification was gradually refined, reaching its apex in Dynasty 21. Some of the techniques that were developed have never been
matched, let alone surpassed, even to the present day. Embalmers removed the organs subject to rapid decay—the liver, lungs, stomach,
and intestines—and embalmed them separately in four containers
called canopic jars. As a rule the heart, understood as the seat of intel-
ligence, was left in the body. In later instances the kidneys were also
left inside.

Not unlike an artist, who by constructing images of human beings and gods from diverse materials creates an additional "body" for them, the Egyptian embalmer used the material of the human body to make a lifelike, lasting image that could be revived and given a new soul at any time. This would occur through the ceremony known as the Opening of the Mouth, which was performed on both statues and mummies to prepare the mouth for receiving food and for speech, as well as to awaken all the other senses so the deceased could enjoy the offerings in the Beyond.

The removal and separate burial of internal organs dates from Dynasty 4; the first record we have comes from the burial of the mother of Cheops. Initially, the organs of the deceased, only minimally preserved in a salt solution, were placed in four compartments of a box; later the box was replaced by canopic jars, which were made of alabaster or limestone. Like the mummy, the canopic jars with their respective organs can represent an image as well as an independent part of the human being. The first such jars had flat lids, but in the First Intermediate Period these were replaced by lids in the shape of hu-

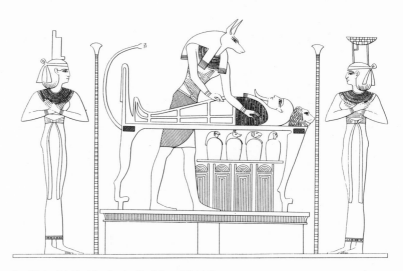

Anubis beside the bier, flanked by Isis and Nephthys;
below the bier are the four canopic jars with
their chests.

man heads, which personified the preserved organs. Some canopic jars from the Middle Kingdom even sport arms and legs to emphasize further the idea of the organs as independent beings. In the New Kingdom the organs were sometimes treated like the corpse itself by being wrapped and placed in small mummy cases of their own. And in Dynasty 18 and thereafter, the jar lids represent the heads of the four sons of Horus (ape, dog, falcon, and human), who as tutelary gods watch over the body and its organs.

Not everything that was removed when the body was prepared for embalming found its way into the four canopic jars. At the same time, however, the Egyptians tried not to let any part of bodily existence be lost; the practice extended even to materials that had come into contact with the corpse. These they carefully assembled and buried separately. The body parts taken out of the corpse that were not placed in the canopic jars were placed in an unusual-looking receptacle called a *tekenu*. The *tekenu* was transported on a sledge pulled by cattle in the funeral procession, together with the coffin and case holding the canopic jars. In pictures the *tekenu* usually appears as a shapeless, sacklike black mass with a human head, which implies that it too stands as both an image of the deceased and an independent being. Earlier scholarship contains less than convincing interpretations of the figure as a human sacrifice or as an echo of a prehistoric corpse in a contracted position. In my view, this formless entity should instead be understood as the sum total of all that the Egyptians could not mummify but still wished to include in the burial ritual so that it too might experience resurrection in the hereafter.

For one to lead a full existence in the afterlife, the Egyptians deemed it essential that one's body be physically intact. They hoped that out of the protective mummy case there would emerge a new, transfigured body, free of all earthly imperfections. Even those large

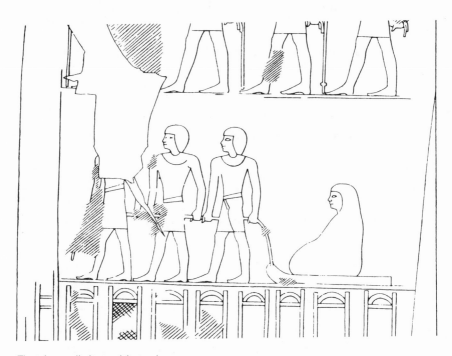

The *tekenu* pulled toward the tomb.

segments of the population unable to afford the elaborate immortalization technique of mummification were confident that in the hereafter, physical existence would continue, although in a different way. As described in detail in the New Kingdom Books of the Netherworld, resurrection was believed to occur in several stages, until finally the deceased emerged with a completely new, regenerated body capable of performing all functions. In this connection we find certain spells in the Book of the Dead intended to guarantee the return of the eyes, mouth, heart, and even the head of the deceased in the hereafter; other spells make it possible for the deceased to stride forth unimpeded.

The tree goddess serving bread and cool water
to the deceased on a Ramesside stela. Museo
Archeologico, Florence.

The material provisions for the body in the afterlife are shown in
the image of the tree goddess. The figure of a goddess growing out of
a tree trunk offers the deceased food and drink. As one hand pours
cool, refreshing water from a container, the other proffers an array of
breads and vegetables spread out on an offering mat. The deceased
catches the water in his hands, and his *ba*, or soul, in the form of a small
bird often drinks together with him. While the generous donor goddess usually remains anonymous, in some cases she appears as Hathor,
"mistress of the western desert," the western Realm of the Dead. At
other times she is the celestial goddess Nut, mistress of the heavens,
the other afterlife realm. In some instances the tree itself serves as her
body, with only human arms and a female breast to indicate the god-

dess who embodies the nurturing forces or bosom of nature, the source of continually new physical and spiritual strength for human beings, even after death.

Detailed offering wishes and entire offering lists give a clear sense of the wealth and sophistication of the material supplies in the Realm of the Dead. For example, it was popular to wish the deceased a thousand different things that included not only foodstuffs but also fabric and clothing, salves, and incense. Cosmetics number among the oldest burial objects; before mummification was developed they were used to preserve or recover the body's fresh appearance in life. The rejuvenated face was then captured and preserved in a bronze mirror, another standard item in the inventory of burial objects.

One of the most important aspects of the Egyptian conception of the body is that its resurrection does not occur only on Judgment Day at the end of time. Rejuvenation and resurrection take place every night in the depths of the underworld, where the deceased once again exercise full power over their bodies. Human beings enjoy a continuous existence interrupted only temporarily by the dissolution of death. This notion contributed a great deal to the relaxed attitude toward the body and its needs. During the Pharaonic Period, there is no trace of asceticism or self-abnegation. On the contrary, the Egyptians affirmed the needs of the body and saw these needs continuing into the afterlife. Although the Wisdom Literature often warned against overindulgence in material pleasures, and the Egyptians practiced both fasting as an expression of mourning and sexual abstinence for religious purification, they never regarded the body as a prison or an enemy of the soul.

In fact, in a certain sense the body was considered divine. The mummy form corresponds to the generalized shape of archaic divine images, and the ascent of the deceased into the world of the gods takes place through the physical body. Further, the ancient theme of member divinization equates each body part with individual divinities. The person is made divine in stages, beginning at the top of the head and concluding with the soles of the feet; in the end, the deceased has become entirely a god, as we read in the Litany of Re, where the dead pharoah addresses the gods as follows:

> I am one of you,
> I have appeared as a vulture.
> My face is a falcon,
> The top of my head is Re.
> My eyes are the Two Women, the Two Sisters,
> My nose is the Horus of the Netherworld.
> My mouth is the Sovereign of the West,
> My throat is Nun.
> My two arms are the Embracing One,
> My fingers are the Graspers.
> My breast is Khepri,
> My heart is Horus-Sunen.
> My liver is the Living One,
> My spleen is the One with the Beak,
> My lungs are the Breathing One.
> My stomach is the Opening One,
> My entrails are the One with the Secret Essence.
> My back is the Weary of Heart,
> My spine is the One on the Bier.
> My ribs are Horus and Thoth,
> My anus is the Great Flood.
> My phallus is Tatenen,
> My glans is the Protected One in Old Cairo.
> My testicles are the Two Hidden Ones,
> My thighs are the two Goddesses.
> My calves are the Two Shining Ones,
> My feet are the One Who Passes Through Mysteries,
> My toes are cobra snakes.
> My limbs are gods,

I am entirely a god,
No limb of mine is without god.
I enter as a god,
And I exit as a god,
The gods have transformed themselves into my body. . . .

It is of no real importance in the Litany of Re which particular body
parts are associated with which divinities, and the comparisons vary in
individual versions, since divinity is only one of two goals invoked in
the litany and guaranteed through recitation of the list. The second
aim is complete physical integrity, as we see quite clearly in later variants that emphasize the ability of all limbs to function properly.

Formally related to the Litany of Re are the Descriptive Songs of
Egyptian love poetry. But when the lover praises the physical beauty
of his beloved he draws comparisons from the natural surroundings:
her mouth is a lotus bud, her breasts are fruits, her arms and forehead
form a trap for birds with her hair as a lure. As long as the context is
life on earth, identification or even comparison with divinities would
be unthinkable: according to the Egyptians, the body does not become divine by virtue of its beauty and perfection. Just the opposite is
true. The physical body attains divinity only when confronting the ultimate threat to its integrity: disfigurement in death. All human
beings are granted a divine existence; it is the form of life associated
with the hereafter.

At the same time that love poetry flourished in the New Kingdom,
the visual arts began to reflect a greater awareness of the sensual ap-
peal of the body. This appreciation notwithstanding, symbolic, abstract representation, in which even the human form is composed of
the same basic shapes, dominated in all periods of Egyptian art. Unlike ancient artists who concentrated on a person's individuality or
beauty, Egyptian artists wished to present the enduring, supraper-

sonal part of the human being that, removed from time, lives on in the hereafter. While not ignoring the physical side of existence, the Egyptians realized that the human being had a variety of spiritual or mental components as well.

Between body and soul stands the concept of *ka*. The word is written with the sign of two outstretched arms that appear to reach upward, but according to Egyptian convention they should be understood as extending horizontally and enfolding the human being in a protective embrace. The *ka* belongs to humans and gods alike; from the beginning of history the term occurs in the names of individuals, and its divine aspect is emphasized by putting the sign on the type of standard usually reserved for images of gods.

Gaston Maspero and subsequent Egyptologists have viewed the *ka* as a kind of double for human beings, created at the same time they were; the idea of a vital force also figures in an understanding of the *ka*. In lists of the fourteen *ka*s controlled by the sun god, we find the following Egyptian definition: "strength, prosperity, nourishment, glory, respect, effectiveness, permanence, creativity, magical power." All these qualities together constitute the multifaceted *ka*, a concept that Thomas Mann describes concisely and elegantly in his Joseph trilogy as "the spiritual body beside the body." In other words, the *ka* represents a bridge between the physical world and the realm of the spirit.

The *ka* is all that enlivens. It is both a life force and the enjoyment of life—or in even more concrete terms well-being and appetite. The vital energy that flows from the *ka* experiences only a temporary interruption in death. Moreover, the new life that continually streams from the *ka* is not restricted to human bodies alone: statues too can contain a *ka*. Without the *ka* there is no life whatsoever. This energy required material provisions; it had to be fed. All nourishment bene-

The deceased burning incense and offering water before his *ka*.

fited a *ka*, and when one Egyptian toasted another he drank "for your *ka*." To ensure continuity between the hereafter and this life, the Egyptians offered their dead as sacrifices "for the *ka*" as well. After death, the human being and the *ka* must reestablish the bond that joined them on earth.

The heart is the source of all forms of energy and all decisions, and like the *ka*, it represents an independent entity. The relation between the heart and the *ka* is therefore close. The heart is the seat of reason and memory, of conscience, desire, and emotion. It is also the source of human free will, which may turn against even the gods and the order of the created world. For this reason the scale found in scenes of judgment balances the heart against a feather, which as a written symbol stands for the ordering principle of *maat*. That the heart represents the entire person in this situation can be deduced from variants of the judgment scene in which a human figure rather than the individual organ appears on one side of the scale.

With a personality of its own, the heart has the ability to forsake the individual, taking will and consciousness with it. According to the Monument of Memphite Theology, "The heart and the tongue have power over all [other] organs . . . for [they] invent and command all. . . . It is the heart that allows every part of knowledge to develop, and the tongue that repeats what the heart has devised." For life after death, therefore, the heart remains the most crucial internal organ. From time to time the Egyptians wrapped the heart separately, as noted above, but they always buried it, unlike other organs, inside the mummified corpse so that it might be accessible to the deceased at all times.

Like the *ka* and the heart, "name" appears as an independent entity. Everything that has been created has a name. In the Monument of Memphite Theology, the creator god Ptah is the "mouth who spoke the name of all things" and thereby ended the earliest time "when not a single thing's name had been spoken yet." At the time of its birth a child receives a name immediately, for without a name the individual does not exist. To prevent namelessness in the hereafter, the Egyptians tried to make their names endure for all eternity. The earliest examples of written language are names.

The name provided an identity ("God is my name," the deceased asserts when entering the world of the gods), and it could also represent the person. This is true particularly of the royal name that stands for the image of the pharaoh on many monuments. Officials prayed before an image of the king, but they might honor his name instead. On the chariot case of Tuthmosis IV, the enemy falls beneath a raised club held not by the pharaoh but by his name. The name of a god, like the name of a king, exuded power that could be enlisted in the service of magic. The name Amun, for example, was an effective type of water magic that rendered crocodiles helpless, and countless amulets bear the name of either the god Amun or the king. Correspondingly, to eradicate a name was to remove all traces of existence, as demonstrated perhaps most clearly in the extreme case of Akhenaton's persecution of Amun. In many cases the pharaoh replaced the name of his predecessor with his own in order to appropriate a temple, tomb, or statue. Thus the identity of many statues has nothing to do with the physical form itself, but instead derives solely from the name appended. The name furnishes the key to the personality; in and through the name it is possible to harm the individual personality.

The name is not an abstract, immaterial entity. As something that can be written and expunged, it belongs to the physical world. In this sense it resembles the Egyptian conception of the human shadow. The shadow is cast not only by the body but also by the soul especially in connection with life after death. Funerary texts consistently mention the shadow together with the *ba* and the body; and in pictures the shadow, together with *ba* birds, praises the sun god or sometimes alights with the *ba* on a mummified body in order to infuse it with new vital energy.

Two main attributes characterize the shadow: it is able to carry and transfer power, and to move with uncanny agility and speed. In contrast to the equally mobile *ba*, however, the shadow does not take to the sky; it remains closely attached to the earth and the physical world. Even the sun god has a shadow, which meanders through the underworld. This idea of the sun casting a shadow carries over into Egyptian architecture in the form of buildings known as "sun shadows." When the shadow of Re or another god falls on the king, it imbues him with supplemental powers, and wherever the pharaoh appears, his head is shaded by a fan of ostrich feathers that serves as both a visual representation and a verbal sign for the shadow itself.

The meaning of the feathers becomes explicit only in the *ba*, which fills the heavy, earthbound body as a spiritual or psychic presence. From the beginning the Egyptians wrote the word *ba* with a stylized representation of the jabiru stork. Over time the fleshy appendage at the base of the stork's beak was transformed into a breast feather, and in the New Kingdom the body of the bird supported a human head. This alteration draws attention to the status of the *ba* as an independent component of the human being; at times human arms were added to reinforce the point. Since *ba* also means "ram," that animal often occurs as an alternative written sign for the *ba*. Notably, the *ba* of the sun god appears with a ram's head—and sometimes even as a bird with a ram's head—on the god's descent into the underworld.

The *ba* is reunited every night with the physical body in the depths of the underworld. In spell 89 of the Book of the Dead the deceased exclaims: "See that my *ba* comes to me from wherever it may be . . .

that it might see its body once more and alight on its mummy!" The spell implies some anxiety on the part of the speaker that the *ba*, circulating like a bird, might not find its way back "to the place it was yesterday," or that it might be forcibly kept from returning to the body. The anxiety is not completely unfounded, for if the deceased is to experience new life, the body must be reunited with the spirit night after night.

The pictorial vignette accompanying the spell shows a *ba* bird with a human head either perched on top of a mummy or hovering above it, and the additional written text recommends that a golden *ba* bird be placed on the dead person's breast so that at least visually the desired union takes place. The same goal is reflected in Dynasty 21 coffin

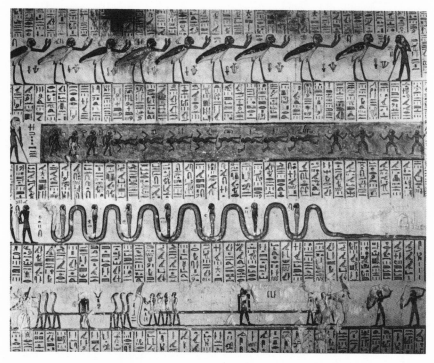

Ba birds offering praise in a scene from the Book of Gates in the tomb of Ramesses VI, Valley of the Kings.

paintings, where the *ba* bird often appears directly behind the head of the deceased, and in Late Period sarcophagi, on which the image of the bird soul hovers over the mummy laid out on the center of the lid. Another example of the reunion motif occurs in the Books of the Netherworld, which represent the nocturnal meeting of the sun god and Osiris as the union of the *ba* (Re) with its body (Osiris).

The majority of references to the *ba* occur in funerary texts. In fact, we rarely meet the *ba* of a living person. Thus, in the story of Sinuhe, it seems quite appropriate that Sinuhe's *ba* and heart leave him during his audience in the royal court after his return home; he loses consciousness and sees death before him until the king speaks to him in a friendly way. In this situation and in a more general sense as well, the *ba* implies consciousness; the *ka*, in contrast, often works from the depths of the unconscious. A Ramesside scribe warns that immoderate beer consumption may result in the loss of the *ba*, for example, and it is the *ba*s of the enemy that flee when they feel threatened by the pharaoh.

The most important document we have concerning the *ba* of a living person is the "Dispute Between a Man and His *Ba*" from the transitional period between the Old Kingdom and Middle Kingdom. In this literary text a man longs for death as a release from what he sees and describes in vivid images as the general incurable misery of the world. His *ba*, speaking as a life-giving principle, counters that he should enjoy life and be of good cheer. After initially threatening to leave the man, the *ba* ultimately proves willing to remain with him forever, even into the afterlife.

The *ba* depends on the body, since it by no means exists as a purely spiritual principle; it has material, physical needs —bread, beer, and everything else the body requires. In a scene from the Book of Gates, the *ba*s receive bread and vegetables "so that their bodies will be

The *ba* as a human-headed bird and the shadow
of Neferrenpet in front of his tomb, from the
Ramesside Book of the Dead of Neferrenpet,
Musées Royaux d'Art et d'Histoire, Brussels.

filled." The *ba* also enjoys the pleasures of love, as we learn from the
many funerary spells that refer to its sexual activity; the union of man
and woman not only is physical but also includes the *ba*.

Freedom of movement and the ability to transform itself into any
shape it wishes are the two basic character traits of the *ba*. Whereas the
earthbound body either remains in its place or, united with the *ba*,
wanders through the underworld, the *ba* may move on its own, as easily as a bird, through sky, earth, and underworld alike. It alone can
leave the hereafter and stroll through earthly gardens. The Egyptians
saw migratory birds as incarnations of the *ba*, since these birds trav-
eled to places beyond the familiar world yet also returned regularly to
that world.

The nocturnal union of the *ba* and the body, in
the Nebensi Book of the Dead.

The *ba* plays a role in every kind of metamorphosis, whereby certain gods and even some animals are considered the *ba*s of others; the four sons of Horus, for instance, also represent *ba*s of Horus. A further distinction is made between *ka* and *ba*: the former embodies the causal principle and the protective power behind a person, while the *ba* signals one thing emerging from another. Thus a son can be the *ba* of his father but not his *ka*; correspondingly, a father can be the son's *ka* but not his *ba*. Re calls Heka, the goddess of magic, his *ba*, yet he himself is a *ba* of the older, primordial god Nun. It is easy to see how the writers of antiquity, confronted with these transformations of *ba*, mistakenly thought that the Egyptians believed in metempsychosis, or the transmigration of the soul. In Christian Egypt, the notions of *ba* and *ka* had lost all resonance, and the Greek term *psyche* came into the language as a loan word for "soul."

Another Egyptian conception of the soul takes the form of a bird: the *akh*. While the term is written with the hieroglyph of a crested ibis (*Ibis comata*), the *akh* does not appear in pictures as a bird. Instead, it is shown always as a mummy, which indicates not merely the physical body, but the more general concept of a divine life-form in the here-after. A person can become an *akh* only after death, and descriptions of the afterlife differentiate clearly between *akh*s, the blessed dead and those dead persons who have been judged and condemned. Related to the Egyptian verb meaning "to illuminate," the term *akh* is usually translated as "transfigured one," for it is through a process of ritual transfigurations that the deceased becomes an *akh*.

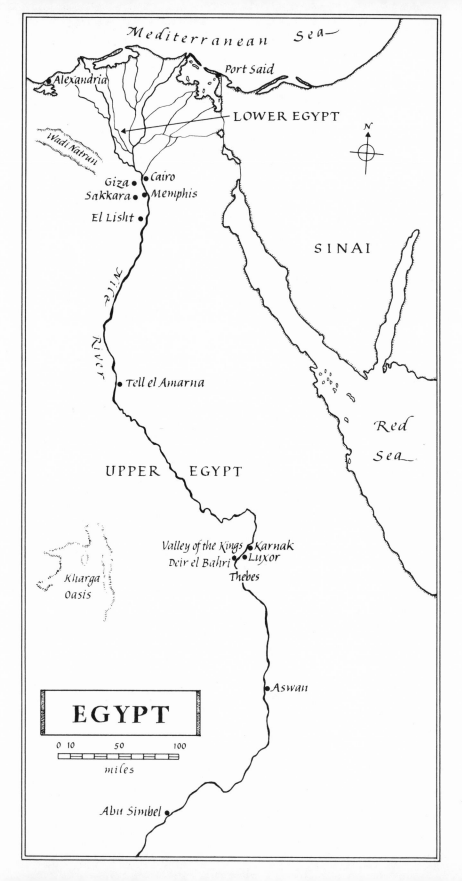

Mediterranean Sea

Port Said

Alexandria

LOWER EGYPT

N

Wadi Natrun

Giza
Sakkara
El Lisht

Cairo
Memphis

SINAI

Nile River

Tell el Amarna

UPPER EGYPT

Red Sea

Valley of the Kings
Deir el Bahri
Thebes

Karnak
Luxor

Kharga Oasis

Aswan

EGYPT

0 10   50   100
miles

Abu Simbel

CHRONOLOGY

Archaic Period c. 3000–2705 B.C.
> Dynasties 1–2

Old Kingdom c. 2705–2180
> Dynasty 3 (Djoser)   2705–2640
> Dynasty 4 (Cheops, Chephren)   2640–2520
> Dynasty 5 (Unas)   2520–2360
> Dynasty 6 (Pepy II)   2360–2195

First Intermediate Period 2180–1987
> Dynasties 9–10 (Herakleopolis)
> Dynasty 11 (Thebes)

Middle Kingdom 1987–1640
> Dynasty 11 (Mentuhotep)   1987–1938
> Dynasty 12 (Amenemhat, Senwosret)   1938–1759
> Dynasties 13–14   1759–1640

Second Intermediate Period 1640–1530
>	Dynasties 15–16 (Hyksos)
>	Dynasty 17 (Thebes)

New Kingdom 1540–1075

Dynasty 18	1540–1292
Hatshepsut	1479–1458
Tuthmosis III	1479–1426
Amenophis III	1390–1353
Amenophis IV/Akhenaton	1353–1336
Tutankhamun	1332–1323
Ramesside:	
Dynasty 19	1292–1190
Sety I	1291–1279
Ramesses II	1279–1213
Dynasty 20	1190–1075

Third Intermediate Period 1075–664

Dynasty 21 (Tanite)	1075–945
Dynasties 22–24 (Libyan)	945–712
Dynasty 25 (Kushite)	712–664

Late Period 664–305
>	Dynasties 26–30

Ptolmaic Period 305–30

Roman Period 30

NOTE: Dates are from the chronology in *Geist der Pharaonenzeit*

GLOSSARY OF DIVINITIES

Aker. Ancient personification of the earth as well as the Netherworld, known since the Pyramid Texts of the Old Kingdom. Depicted as a strip of land with human head or as a double lion or double sphinx with two heads, he is the ambivalent guardian of the entrance to and exit from the Netherworld. He may be either threatening or helpful to the deceased. His role in the Books of the Netherworld, except in the Book of the Earth, is limited, and he did not enjoy an independent cult.

Amun. "The hidden one"; deity usually shown in anthropomorphic form wearing a tall feather crown, but sometimes as ram or as a goose. His cult is attested to first in the Theban district, but he is mentioned earlier as a primeval deity. Preeminent among deities from 2000 to 1360 B.C., he unites all the characteristics of the creator and sustainer of the world.

Anubis. Funerary god usually depicted as a black canine (jackal) or as a human body with a dog's head. The dead pharaoh's mummy was entrusted to Anubis; he thus plays a prominent role as a protective deity in the royal tombs.

Apophis. Serpentine foe of the sun god, embodying the perpetual menace of

‹ The sky goddess Nut and two images of the sun:
one as it is born from her, the other as it
approaches the passage through her body
during the night. Underside of the lid of the
Dynasty 26 coffin of Udjaersen. The
Metropolitan Museum of Art, New York.

disorder to the ordered world. He is a constant threat to the solar bark and, in a never ending struggle, must be continually warded off by magic.

Aton. The disk of the sun; not worshipped as a deity until the New Kingdom, and raised by Akhenaton to the status of the unique, exclusive god, Aton was depicted initially with a falcon's head and later as a sun disk, with rays terminating in human hands. "The great disk" is mentioned occasionally in the Books of the Netherworld, but not as the separate deity Aton; the disk is merely one manifestation of the sun god himself.

Atum. "The undifferentiated one"; both the primeval being and the creator of the world. His mythological origin placed him at the head of the Ennead of Heliopolis, but in later periods he was worshipped as the evening manifestation of the sun god opposite Khepri, the morning manifestation. Usually represented in purely human form, he is a major figure in the Egyptian pantheon.

Bes. General term for various dwarf gods with monstrous faces, often wearing feather crowns and a lion's mane. They are friendly deities who repel evil, especially at the birth of a child.

Geb. Earth god of a more universal character than Aker, and depicted in purely human form. As god of the earth Geb is "hereditary prince" as well as "ancestor" of the gods. Husband of the sky goddess, Nut, he is the father of Osiris. Offerings were made to the dead through him, but he was not worshipped extensively.

Hathor. "House of Horus"; probably the most universal Egyptian goddess. She has the marked characteristics of a mother, and as the "eye of Re," she brings ruin to all enemies. She is shown usually as a woman with cow's horns and sun disk, or as a cow. In Thebes, and especially in the Valley of the Kings, she merges into the goddess of the pharaoh and Isis, losing her specific identity to Isis, but acquiring another role as mistress of the West, and thus of the Realm of the Dead.

Heka. Anthropomorphic personification of magic. Heka is one of the two constant companions (with Sia) of the sun god in the Book of Gates, and is indispensable in the defeat of Apophis.

Horus. Possibly identified with "the distant one," Horus is an ancient god of the sky and kingship. His close links with the sun god and later with Osiris and Isis lead to many new associations, and his martial and youthful aspects become especially prominent. The living pharaoh is Horus, the son and avenger of Osiris; the deceased pharaoh becomes Osiris.

Hu. Personification of the "utterance" with which the creator god calls things into being. With Heka and Sia he is one of the creative forces that constantly accompany the sun god in the Netherworld. Hu is not worshipped.

Isis. Sister-spouse of Osiris and mother of Horus. Her name is written with the sign for "throne." She protects the youthful Horus, but also helps the sun god. She is shown usually as a woman with the "throne" sign on her head, but because of her multiple connections with other goddesses, she is depicted in countless other forms; Isis is thus the "multiform one" par excellence. Her role in the royal tombs is manifold; as the wife of Osiris-the-dead-pharaoh, she protects the pharaoh (in the divine scenes and on the royal sarcophagus); as an independent deity, she accompanies the sun god and has her own place in the landscape of the Netherworld.

Khepri. "He who is coming into being"; morning manifestation of the sun god, usually shown as a scarab beetle, and more rarely in human form with a scarab beetle for a head. Like other prominent deities in the Books of the Netherworld, Khepri appears exclusively in the tombs and funerary literature, without an independent cult.

Khnum. Ram-headed god who was worshipped from the Archaic Period on, chiefly around Elephantine.

Maat. Personification of the "order" of the world established at the Creation, shown as a woman with a feather in her hair. She was considered the daughter of the creator god (Re) and had a widespread cult from early times.

Nefertum. God of the lotus, shown as a human figure with a lotus on his head, and called "lotus to the nose of Re."

Neith. "The terrifying one"; goddess of war and the chase, her warlike attributes (arrows and shield) never far away. Often depicted as androgynous, Neith's main role was that of a primeval goddess, and she was worshipped from the Archaic Period, mainly in Sais and Esna. While her significance outside Sais diminished, her role as divine protector in the Valley of the Kings grew as she joined Selket, Nephthys, and Isis in the defense of Osiris.

Nephthys. "Mistress of the House"; anthropomorphic goddess who accompanies Isis in bewailing and protecting Osiris, as well as in worshipping the sun god. Mythologically, she is the sister-spouse of Osiris's murderer, Seth; the pair have no children, Nephthys supposedly being infertile, (although by another tradition Nephthys reputedly bore Anubis to Osiris). As early as the Pyramid Texts, Nephthys joined Isis in serving the sun god. She plays almost no independent role in myth or cult.

Nun. Personification of the primeval waters from which everything arose, and from which the sun daily emerges, renewed and rejuvenated; hence Nun is "father of the gods." With his female counterpart, Naunet, he forms the first generation of the family group of eight gods (the Ogdoad of Hermopolis). Occasionally depicted in human form, he also assumes a frog's head, drawing on his role as a fertility god. The annual inundation of the Nile was associated with a repetition of the Creation and thus with Nun.

Nut. Ancient goddess of the heavens, depicted as a woman arching over her husband, the earth god Geb. She daily gives birth to and then swallows the sun, and all the other celestial bodies; she also takes the deceased into her protection.

Osiris. This god, who suffered a violent death at the hands of his brother Seth, is depicted anthropomorphically in mummy form without indication of limbs. His attributes of crook and flail allude to his ancient links with the kingship and with pastoralism; other features provide analogies with the death and revival of nature. The most important role of this most complex of gods is as ruler of the dead. The dead pharaoh was himself Osiris. With Isis Osiris posthumously begat Horus. In the Middle Kingdom Abydos was the center of Osiris's cult.

Ptah. Ancient god worshipped in Memphis, where he was regarded as creator of the world and god of technology. Ptah was depicted anthropomorphically, without articulated limbs, but with his hands free before him, bearing symbols of power.

Ptah-Tatenen. Divinity in which the ancient creator god Ptah was joined to the chthonic deity Tatenen.

Re. Most important and common name of the sun god, who is combined with many other gods. He is depicted usually in human form and was worshipped primarily as the creator and sustainer of the world. His bark traverses the heavens by day, and the Netherworld by night. Heliopolis was his chief cult center from earliest times.

Seth. Violent and ambivalent god frequently represented as a fabulous animal (the "Seth animal"), but also as a human with that animal's characteristic head. Associated with the marginal world of the deserts and foreign countries, Seth is engaged in a constant struggle with Osiris and Horus, both of whom symbolize the reestablishment of divine order, and both of whom are his brothers, according to varying traditions. Seth, with Isis, magically wards off Apophis, the serpentine foe of the sun god and symbol of chaos par excellence.

Shu. God of the space separating the earth from the heavens, and of the light in that airy space. Through his separation of earth and sky Shu plays an important role in the creation of the world. He is depicted as a human, sometimes with a feather in his hair; he is represented also with a lion's head.

Sia. Personification of perception who, together with Hu and Heka, makes the world of the Creation possible. With Heka he forms the crew of the solar bark in the Book of Gates.

Tatenen. "Risen land"; embodiment of the depths of the earth. He was combined with Ptah in Memphis from the time of the New Kingdom. Tatenen is depicted in human form, wearing ram's horns and a crown of feathers.

Tefnut. Goddess who forms, with Shu, the first divine couple, engendered by Atum without a female partner. Both Shu and Tefnut are depicted as a pair of lions and Tefnut also appears as the eye of the sun.

Chapter 1.

I have dealt with the topic of word and image in two Eranos lectures: "Hiero-glyphen: Die Welt im Spiegel der Zeichen," *Eranos Jahrbuch*, 55 (1986), pp. 403–438; and "Die Tragweite der Bilder: Altägyptische Bildaussagen," *Eranos Jahrbuch*, 48 (1979), pp. 183–237. From the vast literature on the topic of writing, at least the following should be mentioned: the contributions of P. Vernus in *L'écriture et l'art de l'Égypte ancienne*, ed. A. M. Christin (Paris, 1986); and S. Schott, "Hieroglyphen: Untersuchungen zum Ursprung der Schrift," *Akademie der Wissenschaft und der Literatur in Mainz, Abhandlungen der Geistes- und Sozialwissenschaftlichen Klasse*, 1950, no. 24.

A new German edition of Horapollon by H. J. Thissen is forthcoming; the only other available German translation was done by J. Herold in 1554! Still considered a standard work on Renaissance pictographs and hiero-glyphs is L. Volkmann, *Bilderschriften der Renaissance* (Leipzig, 1923; rpt. Nieuwkoop, 1962). J. Assmann discusses the peace policies of Ramesses II in "Krieg und Frieden im alten Ägypten: Ramses II. und die Schlacht bei Ka-desch," *Mannheimer Forum* 83/84 (1983), pp. 175–231; the image of the destroyed landscape is found in W. Wreszinski, *Atlas zur altägyptischen Kultur-geschichte* (Leipzig, 1935), vol. 2, pl. 35.

Chapter 2.

A monograph on ancient Egyptian conceptions of creation remains to be written. For an overview, see S. Sauneron and J. Yoyotte in the collection *La Naissance du Monde* (*Sources Orientales*, 1; Paris 1959). I touched on individual aspects of the topic in the Eranos lecture "Verfall und Regeneration der Schöpfung," *Eranos Jahrbuch*, 46 (1977), pp. 411–449, and have discussed the "second act" of creation in *Der ägyptische Mythos von der Himmelskuh: Eine Ätiologie des Unvollkommenen* (Freiburg, Switzerland/Gottingen, 1982). See also J. Assmann's article "Schöpfung" in *Lexikon der Ägyptologie* (Wiesbaden, 1975ff.), and his *Re und Amun: Die Krise des polytheistischen Weltbilds im Ägypten der 18.–20. Dynastie* (Freiburg, Switzerland/Gottingen, 1983). The pertinent hymns are found in Assmann's, *Ägyptische Hymnen und Gebete* (Zurich/Munich, 1975).

Chapter 3.

The two main sources for this chapter are J. Assmann, *Zeit und Ewigkeit im alten Ägypten* (Heidelberg, 1975), and my Eranos lecture "Zeitliches Jenseits im alten Ägypten," *Eranos Jahrbuch*, 47 (1978), pp. 269–307. See also L. Kákosy, "Einige Probleme des ägyptischen Zeitbegriffes," *Oikumene* (Budapest), 2 (1978), pp. 95–111; and E. Otto, "Altägyptische Zeitvorstellungen und Zeitbegriffe," *Welt als Geschichte*, 14 (1954), pp. 135–148. L. V. Zabkar gives an overview of earlier differentiations between the concepts *neheh* and *djet* in the *Journal of Near Eastern Studies*, 24 (1965), pp. 77–83. The Vandier Papyrus has been edited by G. Posener in *Le Papyrus Vandier* (Cairo, 1985).

Chapter 4.

The Egyptian attitude toward limits was the topic of my Eranos lecture "Von zweierlei Grenzen im alten Ägypten," *Eranos Jahrbuch*, 49 (1980), pp. 393–

427; the Egyptian treatment of symmetry was the subject of a lecture I gave in 1982 on the anniversary of the German Archaeological Institute in Cairo: "Zur Symmetrie in Kunst und Denken der Ägypter," *Ägypten—Dauer und Wandel* (Mainz, 1985), pp. 71–78. See also the catalogue for the 1986 Darmstadt exhibition on symmetry, especially the article by S. Schoske and H. Brunner, "Die Grenzen von Zeit und Raum bei den Ägyptern," *Archiv für Orientforschung*, 17 (1954–55), pp. 141–145. For more on the phenomenon of the "sloping sky," see W. Westendorf, *Altägyptische Darstellungen des Sonnenlaufes auf der abschüssigen Himmelsbahn* (Berlin, 1966); and on the development of the royal tombs, E. Hornung, "Struktur und Entwicklung der Gräber im Tal der Könige," *Zeitschrift für ägyptische Sprache und Altertumskunde*, 105 (1978), pp. 59–66 (based on a lecture given on May 13, 1976, on the occasion of the reopening of the Egyptian Museum in Leipzig). W. Decker discusses athletic records in "Der Rekord des Rituals: Zum sportlichen Rekord im alten Ägypten," in *Sport zwischen Eigenständigkeit und Fremdbestimmung: Festschrift für H. Bernett* (Bonn, 1986), pp. 66–74.

Chapter 5.
Sources for the New Kingdom are found primarily in E. Hornung, *Ägyptische Unterweltsbücher* (Zurich/Munich, 1972; 2nd ed. 1984), and *Das Totenbuch der Ägypter* (Zurich/Munich, 1979). For more on the destructive aspects of the hereafter see Hornung, *Altägyptische Höllenvorstellungen* (Berlin, 1968). On the royal tombs and their decoration, see Hornung, *Tal der Könige: Die Ruhestätte der Pharaonen* (Zurich/Munich, 1982; 4th ed. 1988; Eng. tr., *The Valley of the Kings: Horizon of Eternity*, New York, 1990); and the Eranos lectures "Auf den Spuren der Sonne: Gang durch ein ägyptisches Königsgrab," *Eranos Jahrbuch*, 50 (1981), pp. 431–475, and "Die Tragweite der Bilder" (see notes to chapter 1) for the scenes of the sun's course. The Abdyos quotations are taken from K. A. Kitchen, *Ramesside Inscriptions*, vol. 2, pp. 333, 336.

J. Assmann writes about initiation in "Tod und Initiation im altägyptischen Totenglauben," in *Sehnsucht nach dem Ursprung: Zu Mircea Eliade,* ed. H. P. Duerr (Frankfurt am Main, 1983), pp. 336–359; since Assmann does not address social aspects (the circle of initiates), the fundamental question of who initiated whom still remains unanswered. This much at least is sure: As was not the case in the Hellenistic Period, pharaonic Egypt knew no mystery cults.

Chapter 6.

This chapter is based on a lecture delivered before the Münster Historical Society on July 2, 1974. For more on the symbolism of the Egyptian temple see F. Teichmann, *Der Mensch und sein Tempel—Ägypten* (Stuttgart, 1978), and R. B. Finnestad, *Image of the World and Symbol of the Creator* (Wiesbaden, 1985), as well as the essay collection *Tempel und Kult*, ed. W. Helck (Wiesbaden, 1987). On the composition of cult scenes, see the important studies by D. Arnold, *Wandbild und Raumfunktion in ägyptischen Tempeln des Neuen Reiches* (Berlin, 1962), and E. Winter, *Untersuchungen zu den ägyptischen Tempelreliefs der griechischen-römischen Zeit* (Graz, 1968). The incorporation of the sun's course into the temple is discussed by H. Brunner in "Die Sonnenbahn in ägyptischen Tempeln," *Archäologie und Altes Testament: Festschrift für K. Galling* (Tübingen, 1970), pp. 27–34; and by E. Graefe in "Der Sonnenaufgang zwischen den Pylontürmen," *Orientalia Lovaniensia Periodica*, 14 (1983), pp. 55–79.

Chapter 7.

The concept of *maat* was the topic of my 1987 Eranos lecture, "Maat—Gerechtigkeit für alle? Zur altägyptischen Ethik," *Eranos Jahrbuch*, 56 (1987), pp. 385–427. The second part of the lecture, which is not presented here, juxtaposes the ideal of *maat* with the ancient Egyptian reality, and addresses both the topic of emotions as disruptions of *maat* and the debate concerning *maat* after Akhenaton. The following works should also be mentioned: R. Anthes, *Die Maat des Echnaton von Amarna* (Baltimore, 1952); S. Morenz, *Gott und Mensch im alten Ägypten* (Leipzig, 1964), pp. 118–140 (2nd ed. 1984, pp. 158ff); H. H. Schmid, *Gerechtigkeit als Weltordnung* (Tübingen, 1968), pp. 46–61; W. Westendorf, "Ursprung und Wesen der Maat," in *Studien zur Sprache und Religion Ägyptens: Festschrift für W. Westendorf* (Göttingen, 1984), pp. 687–701; and W. Westendorf, *Ägypten: Theologie und Frömmigkeit einer frühen Hochkultur* (Stuttgart, 1984), pp. 11–14. The complete Egyptian Wisdom Teachings are now available in German translation: *Altägyptische Weisheit: Lehren für das Leben*, ed. H. Brunner (Zurich/Munich, 1988). See also J. Assman, *Ma'at: Gerechtigkeit und Unsterblichkeit im alten Ägypten* (Munich, 1990).

Chapter 8.

I discussed the Egyptian conception of history in my inaugural lecture in Münster on June 13, 1964, which was published together with the essay "Der Untergang Mexikos im indianischen Geschichtsbild" in *Geschichte als Fest* (Darmstadt, 1966; out of print). See also E. Otto, "Geschichtsbild und Geschichtsschreibung in Ägypten," *Die Welt des Orients*, 3 (1966), pp. 161–176. I have returned to the topic in numerous essays and lectures: "Politische Planung und Realität im alten Ägypten," *Saeculum*, 22 (1971), pp. 48–58; "Zum altägyptischen Geschichtsbewußtsein," in *Archäologie und Geschichtsbewußtsein*, ed. H. Müller-Karpe (Munich, 1982), pp. 13–30; and "Pharao ludens," *Eranos Jahrbuch*, 51 (1982), pp. 479–516. See also J. von Beckerath, "Geschichtsüberlieferung im alten Ägypten," *Saeculum*, 29 (1978), pp. 11–17; U. Luft, *Beiträge zur Historisierung der Götterwelt und der Mythenschreibung* (Budapest, 1978), and D. Wilding, "Geschichtsauffassung," in *Lexikon der Ägyptologie* (Wiesbaden, 1975ff). On the *sed* festival see, E. Hornung and E. Staehelin, *Studien zum Sedfest* (Geneva, 1974); on kingship, M. A. Bonhême and A. Forgeau, *Pharaon: Les secrets du Pouvoir* (Paris, 1988); on material from the Early Period such as the Annals tablet, W. Helck, *Untersuchungen zur Thinitenzeit* (Wiesbaden, 1987); and on other pertinent sources, D. B. Redford, *Pharaonic King-Lists, Annals and Day-Books* (Mississauga, Canada, 1986). It might also be noted that Karl Hauch chose "History as Celebration" as the motto for his publication *Goldbrakteaten aus Sievern* (Munich, 1970).

Chapter 9.

This chapter is a shortened version of the Eranos lecture "Fisch und Vogel: Zur altägyptischen Sicht des Menschen," *Eranos Jahrbuch*, 52 (1983), pp. 455–496. Available monographs on individual parts of the human being include the following: U. Schweitzer, *Das Wesen des Ka im Diesseits und Jenseits der alten Ägypter* (Glückstadt, 1956); A. Piankoff, *Le coeur dans les texts égyptiens* (Paris, 1930); B. George, *Zu den altägyptischen Vorstellungen vom Schatten als Seele* (Bonn, 1970); L. V. Zabkar, *A Study of the Ba Concept in Ancient Egyptian Texts* (Chicago, 1968); E. M. Wolf-Brinkmann, *Versuch einer Deutung des Begriffes "ba" anhand der Überlieferung der Frühzeit und des Alten Reiches* (Freiburg, 1968); G. Englund, *Akh—une notion religieuse dans l'Égypte pharaonique* (Uppsala, 1978). See also E. Hornung, "Vom Sinn der Mummifizierung," *Die Welt des Orients*, 14 (1983), pp. 167–175, based on a talk given at the 27th International Conference of Orientalists, Ann Arbor, Michigan, in August 1967.

INDEX

ILLUSTRATION CREDITS
(keyed to page numbers)